TOBAGO

Come explore the beautiful shores of an island where its diverse and rich culture will take you to places you've only imagined.

Discover
The Rhythm

www.visittobago.gov.tt

TOBAGO
DEPARTMENT OF TOURISM

TABLE OF CONTENTS

TOBAGO'S V.I.P
That's You – Our Visitor

No one's more important to the general Tobago population than you, the visitor. So - hey! thanks for choosing our island, you're in a special place.

In Tobago, Nature has found ways to excel; go find the bounteous beauty in the silences of the forest and tranquil beaches, the gurgling rivers and tumbling waterfalls. Fortunately for you, this bounteous beauty is not confined to terra firma; you'll find all the colours of the rainbow beneath the azure waters of this tropical isle.

Rise with the sun and find the ocean's horizon and you will be seduced by the sunrise that's one of nature's wonders. Find yourself a powdery white-sand beach at sunset and look for the 'green flash' as the sun sinks beneath the turquoise sea - total bliss! Relax, explore and come back again for more. ***Go on, spoil yourself...***

Chapter 1
WELCOME &
WAXING LYRICAL

Today I entered a land where men were tall as trees

I met a distant traveller

and saw a glittering jewel floating through the air!

...I lived a *true* story in the true Caribbean.

Experience the amazing sights and sounds of Trinidad's Carnival or let the beauty of Tobagos sea creatures and rare flora and fauna leave you breathless.
It all happens right here...

CARIBBEAN

My True Story!

TRINIDAD & TOBAGO
THE TRUE CARIBBEAN

A RECIPE FOR TOBAGO CHILL(I)

By Judi — Norfolk, U.K.

INGREDIENTS

A body with a large helping of stress   A portion of overwork
A pinch of British winter aversion   A large amount of fatigue
1 airline ticket to Tobago

METHOD

Combine above ingredients; arrive Crown Point airport. Simmer slowly whilst negotiating Immigration and baggage handling. Arrive at hotel – pour all ingredients (except airline ticket) into a swim suit and head for choice of beach; personally I would recommend Pigeon Point. Allow ingredients to soak up the invigorating sunshine and at frequent intervals, baste with copious amounts of rum.

When heat from the sun has dropped slightly, take ingredients to Sunday School, where it should be slowly stirred in time to the sweet pan music and basted again with decent amounts of rum. You may find it necessary to feed the ingredients occasionally. This can safely be done at any of the roadside eating places. I have found the ingredients respond well to sweet Paw-Paw, Pineapple, Mango, Chicken and Shrimp; in fact, any of the local delicacies have the ability to make the ingredients happy and content. Repeat the above processes for at least 2 weeks (or for as long as possible). The result is amazing – the ingredients have now been converted into a happy, relaxed, healthy, smiling person who can face the world again.

A word of warning however – This process does become addictive and may need to be repeated at frequent intervals.

WHAT DID HE SAY?

By Mark Puddy

"I thought they spoke English here, but I couldn't understand a word he said!"

Well of course not, it may have an English base but Tobagonians speak Tobagonian! This is a language in its own right, a Creole language, not a dialect.

None of this is surprising if you take into account Tobago's history. Firstly, this was a slave island for nearly two hundred years with Africans from various areas brought over as slaves and sold to estates all over Tobago. There were 7 to 8 different African languages being spoken. Next, African languages were banned by slave masters, who expected slaves to speak English. Thirdly, slave masters were mostly Scottish. And there you have it, the English vocabulary used is a Scottish version which has been placed on an African language structure and then spoken with an accent which is all Tobagonian.

'Ah goin' by Joefield boat nah to sih if he ketch anything dis marning'.
'I am going to Joefield's boat to see if he caught anything this morning.'

The present tense is always used, there is no past or future tense, i.e. no - 'ed' 'stew fish' rather than 'stewed fish'. This is directly from the West African languages.

'Is she fault dat he lose he watch last week.'
'It is her fault that he lost his watch last week.'

There is no 'him' and 'her', only 'he' and 'she'.

Listen carefully and enjoy the language of Tobago!

Excerpt from Mark Puddy's Short Story.
British ex-teacher, Mark Puddy is Tobago's foremost hiking and river walk specialist. Take a walk and enjoy his dry wit as you go......
Tel: 792 0594, Email: puddy@tstt.net.tt

STAY SAFE
DON'T BE A MUG ON HOLIDAY

It's sad and it's a shame, but you will find some dishonest people anywhere you go in the world!!

- Don't let your actions or lack of precautions give the 'baddies' any opportunities............ ..**use only licensed taxis with 'H' prefix number plates**. Rent only from authorised Agencies.
- **Avoid the drug scene. Don't drink and drive.**
- **Use Licensed Tour Guides** to visit the rain forest or when hiking. **Avoid dark, lonely roads** for romantic walks.
- **Use the hotel safe**, don't leave valuables in your vehicles and **avoid deserted beaches**.
- **Secure your rooms** when leaving and when inside relaxing. **Report any suspicious behaviour** to either Police or your accommodation provider.
- **Don't pick up hitch-hikers** or take strangers back to your room or villa.
- Be wise, be careful when using an **ATM machine** and **don't accept help from strangers** to access your funds.
- **Don't isolate yourself**, always carry a Mobile phone – rent one from your landlord or buy a local SIM card.

Don't make a mug of yourself; look after your loved ones and your property. It's your responsibility.

Some Emergency Numbers:-
POLICE - 999 OR 211
FIRE & AMBULANCE - 990
LOCAL & OVERSEAS ASSISTANCE – Dial 0 for Operator
BRITISH HIGH COMMISSION - 622-8960/1/2
GERMAN EMBASSY - 628-1630/1/2

HAVE A SAFE AND ENJOYABLE HOLIDAY!

T&T FAST FACTS

WHERE	11° N, 61° W Tobago 21 miles from Trinidad
SIZE	Tobago 30 X 10 miles • Trinidad 65 x 50 miles
CAPITAL	Scarborough - Tobago • Port of Spain - Trinidad
POPULATION	1.2 Million - Indian, African & Mixed races
LANGUAGE	English
GOVERNMENT	Parliamentary democracy overall Tobago House of Assembly
CURRENCY	TT$ dollar approx TT$6 to US$1 approx TT$10 to £1 Pound sterling ABMs - Local Currency Only
TROPICAL CLIMATE	Dry Season - January to May Rainy Season - June to December Average Temperature 83° F (29° C)
RELIGION	Tobago - Mainly Christian Adventists, Pentecostals, Moravians, Baptists, Catholics & Anglicans Trinidad - Also Hindus & Muslins
TRANSPORT	Public Buses - 'H' Registration (Taxis for hire) 'R' Registration (rentals) Vehicles for rent - Driving on the Left Fast Ferries to and from Trinidad - (2 1/2 hours) Airbridge - Hourly flights between the islands
WEDDINGS	3 Days residence required Must have valid passport and return ticket Under 18? Must have written consent of parents 2 Witnesses

Chapter 2
OUT & ABOUT
ACTIVITIES &
ATTRACTIONS

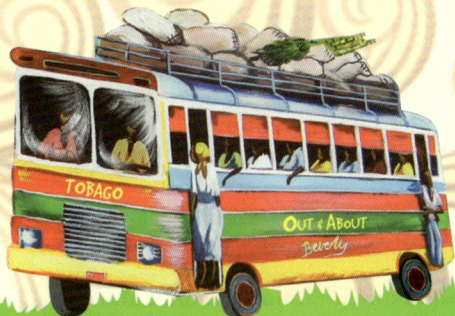

Store Bay
Beach Facility
Welcomes You

TOBAGO

OUT & ABOUT
Beverly

MUST DO'S IN TOBAGO

SEE A TOBAGO SHOW – Heritage Festival/Tobago Jazz Experience/ Culinary Festival, Blue Food Fest etc. Don't miss the goat races...

TAKE A SAIL BOAT OR POWER BOAT TRIP – chart the island's hidden coves.

DO AN ISLAND TOUR – sample the rural delights of the island's villages in a Rental Car or Licensed Taxi.

GO TREKKING IN THE RAIN FOREST – hire a guide and go back to nature.

POWER SHOWER IN A WATERFALL – Argyle Falls is the most popular, but there are many others to seek out.

EXPLORE THE UNDERWATER WORLD OR ENJOY THE WATER SPORTS – scuba dive with one of the many

dive shops or snorkel off beaches round the coast. Wind surf, kite surf, kayak or Jet Ski to your heart's content.

WATCH WITH AWE THE LEATHERBACK TURTLES NESTING ON TURTLE BEACH – from March to August. Join Turtle Watch at your accommodation and be informed of the sightings.

SPEND A DAY AT PIGEON POINT – where else to spend the perfect day on the island's most famous and picturesque beach?

BOOK A TRIP ON A BUCCOO REEF GLASS BOTTOM BOAT AND CHILL OUT ON NO MAN'S LAND – see the corals and reef fish. BBQ fresh fish and relax in the cool, clear waters of No Man's Land.

CHECK OUT STORE BAY FOR LOCAL FOODS AND CRAFTS – eat some crab & dumpling and other local fare. Browse the craft stalls and buy your souvenirs; sunbathe on this delightful beach and stay to watch the sunset.

GO TO SUNDAY SCHOOL – created by the business sector of Buccoo Village to bring trade and gaiety to the otherwise sleepy fishing village. The name is 'tongue in cheek', as most Christian children enjoy the Sunday afternoon tradition of this Victorian religious heritage. Enjoy dinner under a tent from 7 pm, buy carvings and other local crafts and dance to the local steel band and D.J's. All roads lead to Buccoo on a Sunday nite!

MARVEL @ A SUNSET – choose your location for this end of the day treat @ beaches & beach bars around the island.

BUCCOO REEF MARINE PARK

Buccoo Reef is the third largest coral reef in the western hemisphere after those at the Bahamas and Belize. It covers 2.7 sq.miles (7 sq.km) and was designated a marine park in 1973. It is easily accessible by glass bottom boats from Store Bay & Buccoo Bay. Elkhorn coral, star coral, brain coral, fire coral and waving fan and feather corals plus many more turn the reef into a wonderful coral garden.

Situated off the coast of the fishing village of Buccoo, the reef is a unique wonderland of corals, fish and marine life. It is estimated to be more than 10,000 years old. The corals themselves are fascinating as they are animals – not plants. They are made up of colonies of polyps, which have tiny tentacles to catch their food i.e. plankton. There are many different types of coral in all shapes and colours, which create the picturesque sea gardens.

Amongst the coral live over 250 species of multicoloured fish and countless other sea creatures. Stingrays, eels and the endangered Leatherback turtle can be seen there. Unfortunately, coral is very delicate and is easily damaged by pollution and other human activities as well as climate change. Untreated waste water, walking on the corals and boat anchors all cause major damage.

Careful attention is needed to protect this natural wonder and the millions of species that make it their home.

The Buccoo Reef Trust has been established to do just this. *www.buccooreeftrust.com*

Pigeon Point Heritage Park

Where else?

The Pigeon Point jetty with its signature thatched roof shed is as recognisable as Tobago's most famous landmark in much the same way as Tower Bridge represents London or the Statue of Liberty is synonymous with New York.

Tirelessly photographed for television and international magazines, its famous beach was once part of the Bon Accord coconut estate. Notice a profusion of towering palms once you enter its perimeters.

The powdery, white sand beach with its safe, shallow, turquoise waters is every tourist's dream of the ultimate Caribbean scenario. The cresting breakers over nearby Buccoo Reef, the departing occupants of the pastel coloured glass-bottom pleasure boats with white sailed yachts on the horizon, combine to present a picture-perfect vision of an idyllic tropical paradise.

The beach facilities and amenities include acres of manicured grounds to stroll through and explore, bars catering for all tastes, fresh seafood snacks, pizza, burger and ice-cream parlours with ices made from exotic local fruits.

There is also a beachfront restaurant specializing in highly acclaimed local cuisine.

All manner of water sports are available; with an area set aside for wind and kite surfers located at the far end of the beach. At the entrance, by a well-appointed fountain you will find gift shops stocked with local crafts, ceramics and fashionable beach wear.

For an exceptionally modest entrance fee you can safely say upon your return home - *"I've just been to the epicentre of the capital of paradise!"*.

GO SOMEWHERE NICE...

At the Beach
Every Hour is
HAPPY HOUR

...LIKE A TOBAGO BEACH

PIRATES BAY – At the other end of the island and minus beach facilities, it's the ultimate get- away-from-it-all safe hideaway. Romantic access by rowing boat from Charlotteville's sea front. Picnic basket & cooler and you're good to go! Unspoilt, it's a white sandy stunner.

CANOE BAY – Spacious grassy area for toddlers and sporty types, with cabanas to view the sunset at day's end. Very calm and shallow waters ensure a safe environment and with its changing rooms, rest rooms and snack bar it makes for a great stress-free day out, the ultimate unwind. A very modest entrance fee, kids half price. Open daily 'til after sunset.

ENGLISHMAN'S BAY – Great swimming, snorkeling and a backdrop of an

abundance of greenery;
it's earned its accolade for being
one of the best beaches on the planet. Food, drink and crafts on
the edge of the rain forest add to the allure.

Other great beaches are – Store Bay, Speyside, Parlatuvier and
the Jazz on the Beach venue at Mt. Irvine's hotel beach where the
beach facility at the far end do scrumptious local lunches and the
surfing crew's friendly lime create a cool, laid-back ambience.

Stonehaven Bay, a section of the massive Courland Bay, Bacolet
Bay with its black sand and historic hotel and Arnos Vale's quality
snorkeling all add favourably to Tobago's maritime delights.

Bloody Bay, Man O War Bay and the bays at Castara with
Heavenly Bay in particular
are all in the running for
where you will probably
meet someone even
nicer!

BIG-UP THE 'BAGO BEACH...

STORE BAY'S GOT IT ALL...

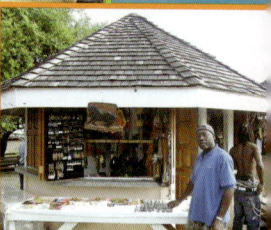

Dalia's Craft Shop #11

THE ALMOND TREE CRAFT SHOP

LIFE GUARD

sand, sea,
sun & fun.

SWEET
TOBAGO BEACHES

Beautiful Beach Babes

Go Visit the Tobago Museum

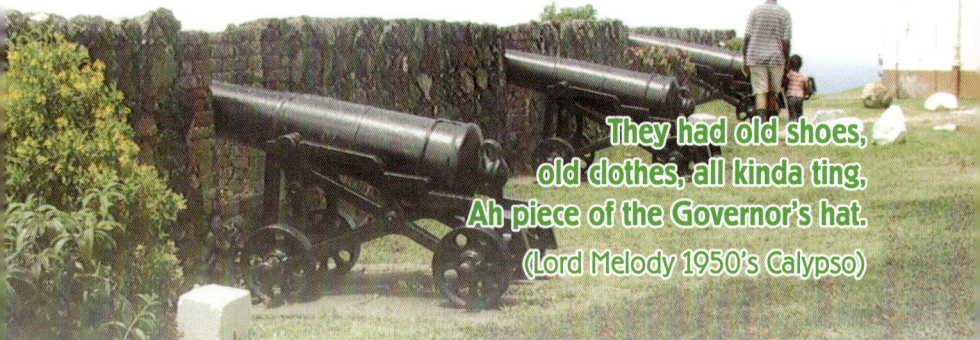

**They had old shoes,
old clothes, all kinda ting,
Ah piece of the Governor's hat.**

(Lord Melody 1950's Calypso)

The museum, housed on two floors, offers and displays information relating to segments of Tobago's history and some areas of the region. It takes you back 300 years and is located at Fort King George up on the hill above Scarborough giving a 360 degree panoramic view of the town beneath as well as the horizons of the Windward coast.

The British Governor General of Grenada and Tobago authorised the erection in 1777 of barracks, kitchens and a parade ground to house two companies of soldiers. Four years later the French over ran the island but work continued under Count Dillon who renamed it Fort Castries in honour of the French War Minister – The Marquis of Castries (hence Castries Street).

The after effects of the French Revolution spread to their possessions in the West Indies, where in Tobago for example, the garrison, having renamed the fort – Fort Republique and Fort Liberty, eventually mutinied. The British recaptured the fort in 1793 renaming it Fort King George after King George III and a garrison was maintained there until 1854.

One may view original site plans which indicate the locations of the main citadel, officers' mess, prison compound, military cemetery, the powder house, water tanks and the hospital and parade grounds.

Artefacts of the indigenous Aboriginals (Amerindians), various maps, charts and military and colonial administrative documents including slave and plantation data are also on display together with paintings, fossils, stamps, coins and historical utility objects.

Ice Cream Can

It makes for a delightful visit, its location offering wonderful photo opportunities and picturesque views. The museum itself has been well maintained with friendly and helpful staff which included the respected curator for many years – Mr. Hernandez who, amongst his other skills and traits is a charming and amiable artist.

The museum is open Mon - Fri 9am to 4:30pm (closed on Public Holidays) and admission prices are very modest with concessions for teens and kids. They also provide assistance to students pursuing research and they arrange group work shops and lectures. Tel: 639 3970

Go back in time and take a walk through Tobago's past. Inform yourself..........

THE BOTANIC GARDENS
Scarborough's Green, Serene Oasis

The Gardens' centenary was celebrated in 1999, as it was eventually established and run under proper government ordinances from 1899. The land, part of a sugar estate called Deal Fair, was acquired from two sisters who took the government to court for an increase on their original offer of one hundred and fifty pounds.

Tobago's Botanic Gardens was part of a network of gardens throughout the colonies, with Kew Gardens U.K. as the HQ, which focused mainly on the economic use of plants that were exchanged regularly between the gardens. For example, cocoa plants from Grenada were sent to W. Africa when their crops became infected. Kew Gardens recruited the first curator Henry Millen, who arrived from Lagos, Nigeria and by 1900 the nursery was open for sales.

Potentially economic plants were grown and the Garden still retains some of the trees planted a century ago. An avenue of Royal Palms, a mango orchard and a variety of ornamental and flowering plants are among its prominent features.

A guide to the plant list when last enumerated in 1989 identified 84 species of trees, shrubs, ornamentals and vegetables.

There were many active springs in the Garden, particularly one, fondly called 'Granny Betty', which provided the water needs of Scarborough residents; unfortunately this spring is almost dried up now.

Henry Millen was buried in the Garden in 1908, but sadly no evidence of his grave remains. However, the tombstones of two merchants of Glasgow can be viewed at the eastern gate steps of the Admin. buildings.

The Gardens are open daily – **Visit and Enjoy!**

LUISE KIMME

Kimme Museum - "The Castle"

In an interview she said, "There is a gentleness about Tobago. It's not like anywhere else, no other island can compare with this, the beauty of nature and its people."

She carves two to three metre-high figures, jazzy dancers, singers, religious and mythological sculptures from wood with chainsaws and chisels. She creates her world with a passion at her mystical museum in Mt. Irvine. Her love for dance, animals and people is evident in all the figures. She in turn is respected and liked by the people of Tobago.

Make time on a Sunday morning 10 a.m to 2 p.m. *($20TT entrance)* or by appointment and visit her museum on the hills of Mt. Irvine. Get ready to be amazed by the body of work and the joy the sculptures emanate.

Born in Bremen, Germany in 1939 Luise has become a Tobago Legend – in her Lifetime! *Go See!!*

www.luisekimme.com Tel: 868 639 0257

HISTORIC SITES

FORT MILFORD - Next door to the Crown Point Hotel and whose garrisons stayed until 1854 to protect the sugar interests, has terrific views over Store Bay with Buccoo Reef and Pigeon Point in the distance and was built by the British from coral limestone in 1777.

FORT BENNETT - Overlooking Grafton Beach with views of the hills above; it's well maintained and offers good photo opportunities of the crashing seas below at Black Rock. Originally built by the Dutch in the 1630's and refortified by Courlanders to protect the Great Courland Bay, it fell into British hands in the 1800's.

FORT JAMES, PLYMOUTH - British built in the 1760's and briefly held by the French for a decade or so before reverting to the Brits; it has magnificent views of Plymouth jetty, Courland Bay and the coastline beyond.

FORT KING GEORGE - The most visited and photographed as well as the favourite photo opportunity for panoramic views of Scarborough, Bacolet and the Windward coast. Built in the 1770's, a garrison was maintained there until 1854. Set on Scarborough's highest point, it now houses a decent sized museum and is a must-see for cruise ship visitors and holiday makers.

FORT GRANBY - Built on the headland between Barbados Bay and Pinfold Bay, it had a relatively short life as it was abandoned in 1787 having been built around 1765 to protect the area which was cited as the Capital of Tobago i.e. Georgetown. It offers marvelous views of the rocky Windward coast and pound waves.

RICHMOND GREAT HOUSE - Perhaps the only remaining Plantation House of a bygone era; built in 1766 the grounds are well laid out with fruit trees and the views of the surrounding forests and mountains are extremely picturesque. Well worth a visit for a glimpse into a past lifestyle.

MT. DILLON - On a hilltop in the village of Runnemede on the Northside Road to Castara, is where Count Dillon, the Administrator of the French forces chose to build his home. Today it's a regular photo stop for its exhilarating views of the North coast and Castara in particular; a truly breath-taking experience.

CANOE BAY - Originally called 'Kanwoa Bay', a large settlement area for the earliest Indian inhabitants where many artifacts from that period were found and handed over to the museum at Fort King George; it was later called Canoe Bay by early English sailors because of the large number of canoes to be seen there in its shallow waters. An ideal place for family picnics, romantic trysts and 'away-from-it-all atmosphere' with smashing sunset views and Crown Point on the horizon.

CAMBLETON BATTERY - Overlooks Man-O-War Bay and Pirates' Bay at picturesque Charlotteville and its two gun operation protected the ships loading in the bays from American privateers in their war for Independence against the British. Not to be missed as a location for stunning views of one of Tobago's prettiest vistas.

FLAGSTAFF HILL - Used as a radar tracking station and listening post by the U.S. Army against German submarines during World War II. It offers amazing views of St. Giles Islands, Charlotteville and masses of abundant green rainforest.

SUGAR MILLS - You will find preserved and/or renovated examples of these historic remains at a few island locations. An easily accessible example can be seen at the Mt. Irvine Hotel, which was the site of the Island's largest sugar estate of over 700 acres.

Courtesy of Mark Puddy

JAMES PARK

Working

This small shaded square lies at the foot of the picturesque House of Assembly building, one block away up the hill from Ciao Café in Scarborough. Previously used as an outdoor market, it has since been dedicated to the memory of one of Tobago's favourite sons, Alphonso Philbert Theophilus James, a working-class man living in the time of the world's first financial meltdown – the Great Depression.

He was so strong and well built that they nicknamed him 'Fargo', after a sturdy, heavy duty truck of that era. Born in Patience Hill in 1901 he grew up in very humble circumstances leaving the island in 1928 to seek employment in the Trinidad asphalt fields beginning as a labouring stevedore. He soon rose to the leadership of the workforce, eventually becoming a contractor providing labour for the company and improving conditions for the workers by unionizing them. He amassed a small fortune and on one of his visits to Tobago after a prolonged absence and while making his way to his Patience Hill home, the public bus service took the full fare but dropped off

Class Hero

A.P.T. JAMES

all the passengers part-way up the hill on the grounds that the road further on was impassable.

Fargo James' protest against this action endeared him to the people of Tobago and led to his election as Tobago Representative to Trinidad's highest Assembly then under Colonial rule. Both islands were being sadly neglected - Tobago more so - and Governor Fargo as he became known in the Council was relentless in his efforts to improve the lives of his countrymen. He spent 15 years in the legislature on the Opposition benches and fought alongside the great Labour leaders Cipriani and Butler.

In 1948, two years after his first election to the Tobago seat he paid his way to London to present a memo to the Secretary of State outlining Tobago's problems and proposing measures to improve the lot of ordinary Tobagonians; he was elected three times as Tobago's rep.

Popular and colourful – a larger than life figure, he was posthumously awarded T&T's highest honour for outstanding public service. His bust stands in the square which is now named after him.

It's a lovely spot to sit on a bench beneath the trees and watch Tobago's world go by.

Enjoy –
Thanks Fargo!

REVEALED... The Mystery of
THE MYSTERY TOMBSTONE

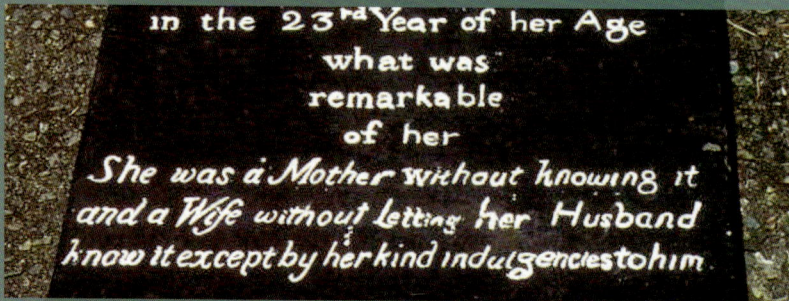

in the 23rd Year of her Age
what was
remarkable
of her
She was a Mother without knowing it
and a Wife without letting her Husband
know it except by her kind indulgencies to him

Betty Scott's father was a substantial member of the island's community and was President of the Governor's Council. A retired military man, he lived at Plymouth in a larger house than the Lt. Governor's residence at Orange Hill and was heartbroken when Betty died on 25th November 1783 as she was his favourite daughter. The distraught father buried his daughter in a corner of his garden. He erected a large tombstone which bore the above inscription.........

Plymouth was a busy port and Betty met and married a boisterous sailor, Alexander Stiven, the son of the master mason who erected most of the original buildings at Fort King George. She became pregnant and died in childbirth – hence the first line of the verse. The second line cleverly tells the reader that Betty was a good wife in that she was not a 'nag' as some wives are wont to be and made allowances for her sailor husband's wanderings as he came and went. Her kind indulgences to him were the obvious outcome of her love for him.

And so Betty Stivens died at the early age of 23 – her unborn child lies buried with her.

Be sure to pay a visit to Betty's tombstone at Plymouth, overlooking the harbour.

SURF'S UP...

@ Mt. Irvine Beach

For many years, in a little corner of Mt. Irvine's Public Beach Facility where nature's forces conspire to produce ideal conditions, local surfing has had a dedicated hardcore of practitioners.

A youthful entrepreneurial spirit has recently led to the establishment of a professional surf school based on the edge of the lively Pleasant Prospect Green run by Dominic Ferdinand, an Oceanography Degree holder who honed his instructing skills in the Canary Islands and amongst this merry band of aficionados are numerous other local enthusiasts. Surfing at Mt. Irvine has no barriers not gender, not age, nothing whatever - all are welcome from novices to world class, locals and foreigners. Even if you do not surf or know the surfing lingo and are just interested in watching the action or chilling under the almond trees absorbing the culture, you are guaranteed to get plenty Trinbago 'ole talk'.

You can book surfing packages that could include accommodation, but there are quite a few traditional providers of accommodation in the Pleasant Prospect and Black Rock areas.

Reward yourself with a challenging Tobago tropical surfing experience.

Cool guys and gals offering a cool scene whenever Surf's up......

Come lime, chill and surf –
Good Vibrations!

www.trinidadandtobagosurfexp.com

TOBAGO DIVIN'
finding the lost garden of eden

Imagine falling asleep and waking up inside a magical world full of colour, set against a crystal clear canvas of inky blue serenity!

Imagine flying on liquid winds, swirling and bubbling in a vortex thick with clouds of plankton and schools of fish, mesmerizing in their variety! Then pinch yourself to make sure that this breathtaking world where fish fly in kaleidoscopic splendour is not just a figment of your imagination.

Then, imagine that dreams really do come true and that in Tobago, they do form the intricate fabric of a fascinating parallel reality.

The volcanic conception of the island has carved in its wake dramatic underwater mountains and ocean pinnacles, which funnel the strong drift currents of South America's Orinoco flow.

Tobago straddles the Atlantic Ocean and the Caribbean Sea and where the two bodies of water converge there is a spectacular variety of marine species nourished by the plankton rich water of the Guyana current.

The fish life is absolutely mind-boggling; all the marine tropicals exist here and interact with many rarely encountered Atlantic creatures.

Tobago possesses an unusual combination of underwater terrains ranging from fine traditional coral reefs to rocky outcroppings encrusted with dense low profile coral and colourful sponges. Here the fish seem larger and more profuse. Encounters with large blue water pelages are frequent, thanks to a natural thriving food chain able to support a hefty population of alpha predators.

Visibility is excellent in the dry season (Jan-July), often reaching in excess of 100 feet. These sought after aquarium-like conditions expose packs of marauding Barracuda, cruising their undersea realm like stealth bombers shadowing a target. Other pelagic include giant Tarpon, which emerge eerily from cloudy surf, an inverted sky where topside waves bathe the rocks in relentless turmoil. Then there are the Devilfish - mystical Manta rays that soar through the endless blue space and feed on the vast planktonic soup, as do the whale sharks and the occasional pods of Sperm and Humpback whales.

A stunning array of smaller creatures completes Tobago's broad spectrum of marine species. Lobsters and Moray eels swarm over shallow coral gardens and steep fringing reef slopes. Frog fish, Scorpion fish, Seahorses and Bat fish blend perfectly with their environment. Reefs vary from shallow beginner dives to vertical walls swept clean of sediment by brisk underwater winds. The drift diving here is second to none and currents often exceed dizzying speeds of eight knots as they propel divers on exhilarating thrill rides across miles of virgin reef territory.

The most unique feature of Tobago's world class diving must be the unpredictable nature of its primal thrills. When in the right place at the right time, you may encounter the most magnificent beasts amongst stunning beauty in a world so grand that you may seldom or never experience it again. You never know when a school of Hammerhead sharks will appear out of the electric blue, humbling spectators in a seemingly endless procession of grace and majesty. These giants are most often found circumnavigating the 'Sisters', - a rugged cluster of ocean pinnacles that tower above the waves emerging from the depths of the sea, one mile off Tobago's Caribbean coast.

These rugged outcroppings offer precipitous cliffs, sheer vertical walls, and numerous pelagic species, including turtles, dolphins and sharks.

The wreck of the M.V. Scarlet Ibis is another popular attraction for divers visiting Tobago. This 350 ft. cargo ship rests upright in 100 feet of clear water. Blanketed with sponges and other decorative soft

corals, she creates a photographer's underwater dream studio complete with resident Barracudas, Cobias, Jew fish and Stingrays.

Other recommended dive sites include 'The Shallows', a tremendous ocean plateau several miles out from Tobago's southwest end. Here Neptune's breath accelerates the Atlantic drift over this impressive tabletop terrain where low profile coral and sculpted sponges provide a feeding ground for some of the most impressive undersea wildlife found anywhere.

Last, but certainly not least, is a diver's utopia where one will find the world's largest recorded brain coral. Speyside is surely what must have become of the Garden of Eden when the great floodwaters covered the globe.

So, if you are searching for some of the most spectacular diving on the planet, there is only one way to discover the truth about this sublime marine paradise. You've heard the rumours; now discover the secret. **Drop everything and go 'Tobago Divin'!**

Article courtesy John Procope, Dive Master - Scuba Adventure Safari.

LIMES & LIMEYS

During the 18th Century sailors in the British Navy spending long periods at sea were prone to suffer from scurvy – a fatal disease. A Naval surgeon discovered that if the sailors drank a daily ration of lime juice, the sickness was kept at bay. British sailors were henceforth known as 'limeys'.

Here is a traditional recipe for your own Rum Punch

1 Measure of Sour (Lime Juice)
2 Measures of Sweet (Grenadine Syrup)
3 Measures of Strong (Rum)
4 Measures of Weak (Fruit Juice)

Add a dash of Angostura Bitters and grated Nutmeg

LIMING
Is a Trinbago ting!

It's a verb, but can also be a noun...............you go out to 'lime' or you can go and have a 'lime' and believe you me, neither has anything to do with that little green citrus fruit you find beside your fish dish!

The origin of the word is perhaps lost in the alcoholic mists of time, but one thing is certain – Trinbago folk just love to do it!

It's the pastime otherwise known as 'hanging out' or 'chilling out' and Trinbagonians have developed it to a fine art. Trinis come over for a Tobago lime, or an outing to the beach with friends can be described as a beach lime; popular bars offer an 'after work lime', particularly on a Friday afternoon/evening. It's a local form of 'de-stressing' or relaxing in the company of friends and colleagues or even strangers if the venue is the 'lime'.

So next time a local says to you – "Come and have a lime", expect to spend a couple of hours doing nothing more daunting than downing a few beers and passing time shooting the breeze in a relaxed and pleasant way.

The word has passed into every day usage and it's taken so seriously that some bright spark came up with a slogan for a T Shirt logo – *"If the job gets in the way of the lime – leave the job".......*

Now there's passion for you!

Some regular liming spots on the island include 'Bago Beach Bar, Colours Bar, Shutters Bar, After Hours, Sundowners, Green Shop Bar, Smilio's, El Pescador and Captain's Bar in Buccoo; IOMA & Bar Code on the Esplanade & Ciao Cafe in S'bobo. Also Limelight and Moon over Water in Pleasant Prospect.

BIRD FEEDING TIME...

Arnos Vale Hotel's
daily afternoon teas at
4 pm bird feeding time
has been an attraction
for many years.

BEING WITH HORSES

Veronika Danzer La Fortune was born in Germany and became a professional equestrian performer in a travelling circus that traversed the European Continent with a herd of 65 horses. Consequently, she visited T&T and fell in love with the people (she married one) and especially with Tobago where she settled in Buccoo.

A fellow artist told her about a horse in Speyside that needed a loving home. Veronika walked the lonely horse from Speyside and so began her extraordinary journey in sharing the world of horses with the villagers, their children and also the island's visitors. They now have 5 horses stabled on the seaside edge of the village.

The sea has always been at the very heart of Buccoo Village life; the provision of fresh fish and having the famous Buccoo Reef on its doorstep as well as its long white sandy beach. It's an invigorating experience to take a horse ride in the shallow sea – good for horses and riders and a lovely sight to see.

With her cheerful outgoing personality, Veronika has expanded her vision to create a charitable arm 'Healing with Horses' that provides free horsemanship skills for the village kids as well as the establishment of an annual summer camp with creative activities for the youngsters.

Volunteers, both local and international have begun to be attracted to this unique project that teaches *"True growth in horsemanship can parallel personal development, whereby wisdom, patience and courage increase through horse interactions and in turn improve them."*

www.being-with-horses.com
www.healing-with-horses.com

KIDS

HOORAY – SCHOOL'S OUT!!
WHISTLING FOR THE WIND

Round my way, the overhead wires display their prisoners – hanging entrails and skeletons of kites they have captured from the local boys' hand-made aerodynamic wonders.

Every part of the kite is the product of ingenious recycling; they need buy nothing except a reel of cotton thread from the local variety store (having plundered Mum's sewing basket).

The fronds of coconut trees provide the ribs which make up the frames of the kite and plastic carrier bags are used to cover the frames and make the tails. Though summer is not ideal kite flying weather (Christmas is). the local boys will *whistle for the wind* (there's a 2 note melody which is meant to summon the wind) and rustle up a kite in the twinkling of an eye – that is if they aren't out and about scrumping mangoes or plums or down on the beach digging in the sand for sea cockroaches to use as bait at the end of a bamboo fishing rod.

Your kids will take home wonderful memories of carefree days filled with the excitement of new experiences.

The Annual Flying Colours Kite Festival takes place usually on Boxing Day, anyone can participate.

ROVANEL'S RESORT in Bon Accord has a small collection of local wildlife on its spacious grounds – feeding time is around 4 p.m and there is a Restaurant/Bar for drinks & snacks. Stop by at Reception to ask permission. Tel: 639-9666/0652

FORT KING GEORGE MUSEUM open weekdays for excellent displays of historical and Amerindian artefacts; educationally rewarding and the best views/photos. Tel: 639-3970

ENVIRONMENT TOBAGO & BUCCOO REEF TRUST located behind Tambrin Radio in Upper Scarborough and Carnbee Junct respectively, Both voluntary organizations have activities for youngsters. Afterwards reef and rainforest tours will make a lot more sense. Tel: ET 660-7642 and BRT 635-2000/631-1623

DWIGHT YORKE STADIUM & LOCAL SPORTS GROUNDS see a football match at the Stadium or have a kick-about at any Village playing field island-wide. Call the Sports Division on 639-2071 or Stadium on 639-3526/4673.

HORSE RIDING contact Being with Horses at Buccoo Village Tel: 639-0953, Friendship Stables Tel: 660-8563.

See www.whatsonintobago.com for latest news on events and leisure activities.

TOBAGO COCOA ESTATE - CHOCOLATE HEAVEN

A Gift from the Gods

The Maya Indians believed that cocoa beans were a gift from the gods and the bitter produce was reserved for the top echelons of their royalty. Its usage spread to Europe and today Swiss chocolates are as famous as Swiss bank accounts and are the basis of a multi-billion dollar industry. Amazingly, not a single cocoa tree can be found growing in Switzerland!

Fortunately for everyone, the company 'Tobago Cocoa Estate' has begun to revive the cocoa industry and it's now possible to tour their working estate on the road to the left of the Argyle Water Fall car park.

You can see the remains of old cocoa houses in Tobago opposite the Beach Facility at Charlotteville and the restaurant at Footprints has a restored roof which glides on rails to enable the beans to either dry with the sun, or be hastily covered at the first sign of rain.

They grow three of the Finest varieties of cocoa in the World. The **Trinitario** variety is only used exclusively in the making of the finest quality chocolates and is never used in the production of common candy chocolates.

At Tobago Cocoa Estate W.I. Ltd they are marring old cocoa traditions with new cocoa technology by planting new Trinitario strains and tapping into some of the best "cocoa minds" in T&T!

Book a tour with Yes! Tourism and fulfill your Chocolate Fantasy!
www.tobagococoa.com

Crown Point
Beach Hotel Limited

TOBAGO'S GRANDE DAME

Major-General Richard Rohmer, a highly decorated WWII fighter pilot, and now a best selling author, is a regular guest and describes the Hotel as his favourite place in all the world.

He's not alone in expressing these sentiments. The list of eminent persons who've stayed here is as long as the proverbial arm, and reads like a who's-who of the past millennium.

Queen Elizabeth II heads the British royalty list. Her honeymooning sister Princess Margaret, dazzled all before her and wittily observed that the shallow waters of the reef were as clear as the new invention nylon - thus NYLON POOL. The world's richest man at the time, John Paul Getty, together with a host of West Indian Prime Ministers, Governors and Governor-Generals all took their rest here. The great entertainers, the Beatles, Nat King Cole, Sammy Davis Jnr. and the legendary Mighty Sparrow together with film stars Robert Mitchum, Margaret Rutherford, John Mills and Walt Disney all slumbered here on their comfortable pillows. The giants of West Indian literature V. S. Naipaul and Derek Walcott must have had a few creative thoughts while gazing out to sea, I'd like to think.

cont'd over

Yet, in spite of its celebrity connections, the Grande Dame welcomes all those who walk through her doors and treats everyone like royalty. The now deceased general manager Neil Vilain looked after the great lady for over 20 years.

For many years, the grounds and the facilities were home to the friendliest regatta, the Angostura Sail Week in May, which is a major event on Tobago's Calendar. So too are the popular Carib

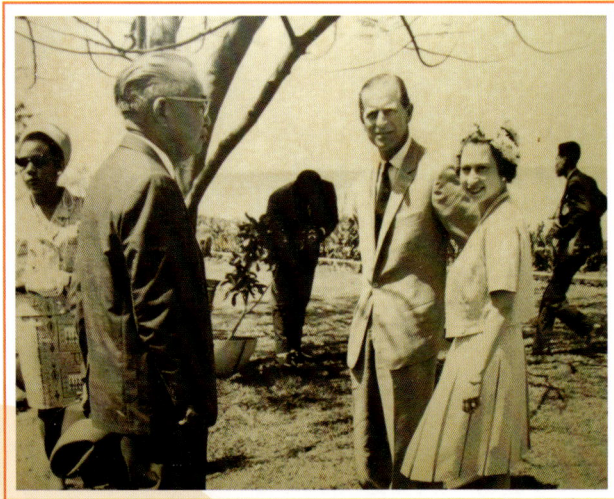

events – the Fishing Tournament and the Great Power Boat Race both head-quartered at the hotel.

Crown Point's Grande Dame sits majestically on 7 acres atop Store Bay's white sand beach and is an ideal base from which to explore this friendly island as most activities can be organised from the Hotel. The Crown Point Beach Hotel was built around 1961/2 just in time for Tobago's worst ever hurricane Flora to come along in 1963 and demolish its top floor!

It's ideal for families and children play freely in the grounds. Recreational facilities include tennis courts, swimming pool, and shuffleboard, while swimming, snorkeling and scuba diving in the crystal clear waters of Store Bay are on the doorstep. You can even kickback and try your hand at fishing right from the grounds.

The Main Building

In Glorious Technicolour
BLUE HAVEN HOTEL

Originally built on a point surrounded on three sides by the sea, the Hotel was extensively renovated and reopened in Dec. 2000. It restored and retained the traditional aspects of its former movie days when Hollywood Royalty chose its ambience as the location for its star-studded production.

Film giants Bob Mitchum and the raven haired actress Rita Hayworth

on the set of Fire Down Below (1957)

slept there and frolicked on its beach when making the 50's classic 'Fire Down Below', a promotional vehicle for rising Calypso music sensation, Harry Belafonte.

Main Building Over the Beach

cont'd over

The English beauty Deborah Kerr, Jack Lemmon and James Mason all featured in the productions of 'Fire Down Below' and 'Heaven Knows Mr. Allison'. Disney's classic 'Swiss Family Robinson' starring child actress Hayley Mills also utilised the hotel's facilities and beautiful scenery.

Wellness Facilities

Located on 15 acres in the upscale neighbourhood of Bacolet, a short drive from Scarborough, the Hotel's modern restorations include all the grandeur and comfortable amenities you would expect in the No. 1 rated get-away. It was also voted as one of the 'Most Romantic Hotels' this side of Paradise.

A gracious colonial style Restaurant serving exquisite gourmet cuisine accompanied by tasteful music, a No-Problem Beach Bar & Restaurant, tennis, manicures & massages, cocktails on the terraces at sunset – you'd feel like a movie star yourself once you enter this delightful Hotel with its adventurous past and historic surroundings.

Blue Haven Beach Bar

The quotation from Conde Nast Traveler sums it up very nicely – "As lovingly restored as a vintage film. Elegant rooms overlook the sea – the view is pure Technicolour".

BLUE HAVEN HOTEL

Chapter 3
Eco Stuff

TOBAGO'S BIOLOGICAL DIVERSITY
Biodiversity

It's a term that's used to describe the variety of life on earth in all its forms and the diverse kinds of habitats or ecosystems in which they're found. In Tobago's case these are the tropical rain forests, wetlands and mangroves and the marine ecosystems which include the popular coral reefs.

Due to the fact that aeons ago Tobago was once connected to South America, many of the flora and fauna of the mainland are to be found here. Because of the volcanic separation of the land mass, many species of life forms are found nowhere else but in Tobago! The island has been blessed with a rich species biodiversity that includes over 210 species of birds, 17 bats, 16 lizards, 21 snakes, 14 frogs, 80 tropical reef fish and 3 endangered sea turtles.

T&T has a system of national parks and laws which promote conservation of biodiversity as many plant and animal extinctions can take place on islands like Tobago.

Environment Tobago is a non-governmental organization that actively promotes public awareness and education about our natural environment.
www.environmenttobago.net

ANCIENT SURVIVORS

About 300 million years ago, early land animals had split into two major groups – Amphibians, which lay eggs in water and breathe partly through moist skin surfaces and Reptiles, which do not need to live near water, have waterproof skin and lay their eggs on land. Most large Marine Reptiles became extinct about 65 million years ago, leaving just Turtles and Crocodiles still living today.

Together with Fish, these groups, known as "Lower Vertebrates" illustrate life's transition over hundreds of millions of years, from a watery existence to a life on land. Many strange deep-sea creatures exist that are unlike anything found nearer the surface, while the World's largest Lizard, the Komodo dragon's bite is so deadly, that its prey dies of blood poisoning.

There are as many Fish species alive today as all the Birds, Reptiles, Amphibians and Mammals put together.

The crab you find in your 'crab & dumpling' would have been caught in the mangrove swamp.

Mangroves thrive in mud – they are often found in coastal areas behind off-shore coral reefs. Their prop or stilt roots are their most noticeable feature as well as their ability to germinate in salt water. Crustaceans like oysters, mussels, barnacles and conch are permanent residents of this habitat. Herons, Egrets and Ibis feed on crustaceans on the ground, while above in the tree canopy you'll find the Iguana, tree-boa snakes and various spiders and insects. The Caiman alligator can also be found. Lobster, Shrimp and some fish species use the mangrove to breed and raise their young. Mangrove swamps protect the land from erosion by reducing the tidal currents and can act as a buffer during storms and is a major filter system for water entering the sea. Wetlands are under pressure from development, over hunting and over fishing and today it is claimed that less than 1% of Tobago is covered by wetlands.

THE MANGROVE

Swampy Nurseries

The mangrove is an ideal place for a nature tour or wild life photography. There are four major wetlands in Tobago at Petit Trou, Kilgwyn, Bon Accord and Buccoo, but others can be found at Courland Bay, Friendship, Louis D'or and Parlatuvier.

Petit Trou at the Tobago Plantations has a wooden walkway through the mangrove which is great for photos and close-up views of these unusual plants, without getting muddy feet.

With thanks to Environment Tobago

CONCHS
(Pronounced - Konks)

The Conch shells you find for sale almost everywhere belong to the Queen Conch, one of five species found throughout the Caribbean region and which is the 2nd largest species of the Stombus snail family. In all, there are approx. 72 species living in tropical seas throughout the world. The smaller shells, usually without the flared lips of the adult conchs, belong to the juveniles harvested indiscriminately from the sea bottom by persons eager to make a quick tourist buck. Adult conchs are over fished for their meat and shells.

The mainly calcium shell is formed from a secretion produced (by all snails) to protect the body tissue. The flared lip shows that the conch has reached adulthood, which takes about 3 years of an average life span of 6 -7 years.

Conchs are vegetarians, feeding on algae and begin life as a pinhead sized hatchling from a well camouflaged egg mass that looks like a lump of sand. It drifts in a sea of plankton for about 3 weeks after which it sinks to the sandy bottom where it buries itself for about a year and metamorphoses into the recognizable tiny shape of a baby conch.

Conchs congregate in groups of similar size and age and are known to bury themselves in the sand during bad weather. They tend to inhabit shallow clear seas and feed through a proboscis-like organ, scraping food into it. Two stalks with alert eyes at their tips lay either side of the proboscis. The horny claw-like foot provides locomotion and is the source of the firm white meat that's high in protein and which ends up on your dinner plate.

The female conch can and does store male sperm, using the previous partner's to fertilize the spawn of over a quarter million eggs. It's a rare occurrence, but pearls have been known to form and grow within the conch, but they are not as valuable as oyster

cont'd over

pearls as they do not retain their colouring.

Man is the conch's main predator; in their natural state they are prey to very few others. The octopus can use its venomous bite to paralyse and pull the adult conch from its shell and the loggerhead turtle's strong jaws can crush its shell; the stingray can flip it up-side-down and bite off its foot.

Nowadays, perhaps the most enduring images of the conch shell are the local cricket fans trumpeting their team's efforts on the field in these calypso-cricket islands.

With the advent of mass tourism and without the protection of legislative conservation it would appear that the days of the conch may very well be numbered.

SOME FACTS ON
FLIPPER THE DOLPHIN

Dolphin hunting is not the norm in T&T. In fact, they are considered 'protected animals' under the Conservation of Wildlife Act, which states that..."no person shall hunt or shall be a party engaged in hunting any protected animal."

Catching, killing or eating or being in possession of whale and dolphin parts is illegal in T&T.

Dolphins are mammals; they are not FISH. They have red meat and live relatively long lives having on average a 20 year life span. An adult female does not reproduce until she is between 10-13 years old and the male is 12-14 years old before being capable of reproduction. They have one baby every few years and they spend a lot of time and energy bringing up their babies. For the first year, the babies feed only on their mother's milk and they are nursed for 2 years.

Good to know.....

cont'd over

'Auntie' dolphins, either male or female may assist with the birth at calving time and are generally the only other dolphins allowed near the calf. When a new baby dolphin is born it immediately heads for the surface of the water for its first breath. The average calf is a little over 3 ft. (1 metre) at birth and can grow to just under 3 metres or 9 ft long. A mother dolphin may whistle to her calf almost continuously for several days after giving birth, in order to help the calf later on to locate its mother by this method of acoustic imprinting.

Thought to be one of the most intelligent and beautiful creatures in our oceans, these warm blooded mammals belong to the group of *Cetaceans* which also encompass all whales and are some of the most highly intelligent creatures on earth. We see them jumping, playing and even hear them laughing as they have fun in the seas. *There are tales of dolphins offering aid to sailors swept overboard or injured swimmers and surfers.*

There are 67 total species of dolphins, with 32 of them being oceanic. River dolphins and porpoises are among whales which make up the other species. Porpoises are often confused with dolphins which have rounded interlocking teeth; porpoise teeth are square. Bottlenose and Spotted dolphins are the varieties most common in these waters.

They live in groups (pods), adult males rarely associating with teenage males (familiar or what?)

Their predators are generally various types of sharks, whales and disease such as bacteria and parasites. Pollution in coastal areas is also responsible for the deaths of large numbers of these complex and amazing creatures.

Boat Tours invariably offer a chance to enjoy the dolphins frolicking in the wake of the boat. Take a trip and perhaps you will be lucky enough to experience them at play.

www.environmenttobago.net

THE SERGEANT MAJOR
REEF FISH

When Dad becomes Mom

He's easily identified by his blue background colour and his 5 vertical black stripes.

You're likely to find him loitering around a purple-green spot in a flattish area of the reef. The spot he's guarding is his eggs – thousands of them, which his lady has deposited in the sand, having encouraged her to do so with his courtship dance and which he subsequently fertilized. He then chases her away, as his maternal instincts take over and he begins to guard his spawn for a week or so until they're hatched and leave home.

The cycle begins all over again as the dad with the mother complex begins clearing his nest site in preparation for his next set of youngsters. ***Look out for him on your snorkeling expeditions.***

LIZARDS & SNAKES

Tobago is a perfect environment for lizards and snakes. 16 species of lizard inhabit the island with at least one, the tiny Ocellated Gecko being found nowhere else. Daytime lizards include the largest new world lizard, the Iguana up o 4 ft. (1,000mm) long, vivid green or striped, often to be seen crossing roads or basking in the sun; the Matto, a large heavy ground lizard around 2 ft. (580mm): Anolis, with its striking yellow throat display; colour changing Chameleons; Teiids and large iridescent ground lizards are often seen crossing lawns; Foot Shaker, vivid green with a habit of waving its front feet, and found in dryer sandy areas; Skinks, found in damp leaf mould; Microteiids or worm lizards, long and snake like. At night various Gecko can easily be seen hunting insects on walls around lights. In the rivers around Hillsborough dam lives the world's smallest alligator – the 3m long Caiman only found in Tobago.

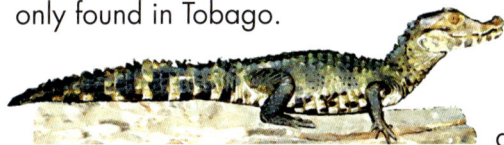

Although there are 21 species of snakes (3 are endemic) none are venomous. The largest is the 12 ft. (3.72m) Boa Constrictor, which is found in the depths of the rainforest. Snakes range from the mighty Boa to the 3m long Cribo, Fiddle String snake, Cat Eyed night snake, Whiplash snake, Doctor Snake, Coffee snake with its collared neck, Cloudy snake and the peculiar Worm snake only found in T&T.

For more interesting info on Tobago see Amazing Tobago Souvenir Map by Phil Dobson Avl. Penny Savers Liquor Dept. and Gift Shops.

LEATHERBACK TURTLES & TURTLE NESTING

Turtles have existed for over 65 million years and were around when dinosaurs roamed the earth.

Tobago is famous for having one of the few nesting beaches for the critically endangered Leatherback turtle, the largest marine turtle weighing up to 900 kg. and measuring up to 8 ft. (2.48 m). Females can take 15-25 years to reach maturity. At night, mainly from March to July, sometimes through to September, they can easily been seeing pulling themselves onto the Caribbean beaches to dig their nests and lay their eggs, covering them and disappearing back into the sea. Leatherbacks are highly migratory, traveling thousands of miles and can dive thousands of feet deep. They eat only jellyfish and other soft-bodied sea organisms. The eggs take up to 60 days to hatch and the baby turtles head straight for the sea.

The Hawksbill turtle, also critically endangered, frequent these waters and nest on the beaches. Much smaller than the Leatherback, but still weighing up to 200 lbs. and 2 1/2 ft. in length it is the most tropical sea turtle remaining in the warm tropical waters all of its life. Green turtles weigh 300–400 lbs and grow to approx. 4 ft. in length. They inhabit the warm shallow waters feeding on seagrass.

Some of Tobago's hotels organize a turtle watch at this time and the conservation group **Save our Seaturtles Tobago (Tel: 357 2862 or info@sos-tobago.org)** is a good bet to contact in the event of you wanting to witness this amazing sight. Bright lights, noisy groups etc. are not welcome at this time.

Yum!

Courtesy Lulu the Leatherback Turtle – by Sonia Canals & Amazing Tobago Souvenir Map Avl. Penny Savers Liquor Dept. and Gift Shops.

FISHERIES ACT # 39 of 1916 – Amended 1975

(i) *No person shall kill, harpoon, catch or otherwise take possession of any female turtle which is in the sea, within any reef or within 1,000 yards of the high water mark of the foreshore where there is no reef.*

(ii) *No person shall take or remove or caused to be taken or removed any turtle eggs after they have been laid and buried by a female turtle or after they have been buried by any person.*

(iii) *No person shall purchase, sell, offer or expose for sale or be in possession of any turtle eggs.*

(iv) *No person shall between the 1st day of March and the 30th day of September kill, harpoon, and catch or otherwise take possession of, purchase, sell, offer or expose for sale any turtle meat.*

Birds of Tobago

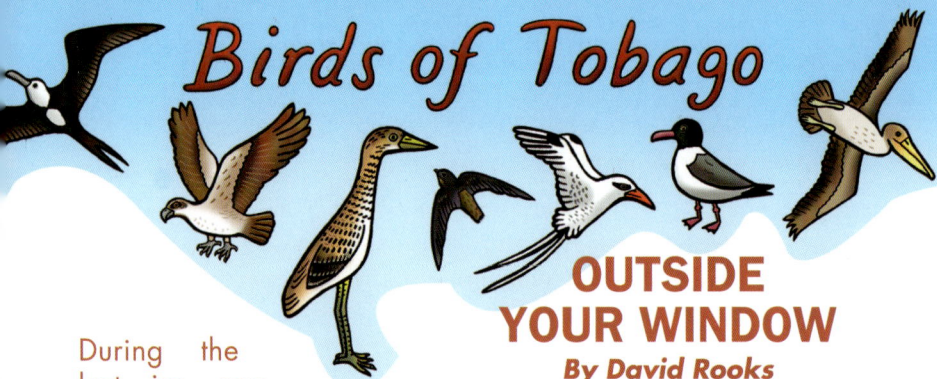

OUTSIDE YOUR WINDOW
By David Rooks

During the last ice age, Tobago was part of South America, human beings making hardly a footprint. Birds evolved. There are, today, 210 species of birds in Tobago.

You will hear them whistling, even at night. I hear the haunting call of the Common Potoo and at dusk and dawn, the Chachalaca, our national bird.

Go anywhere and you will see the Blue–Grey Tanager a flashing and eye-catching blue and be entertained by the most melodious whistling of the Tropical Mockingbird. Look on the overhead wires and see the King Bird, while the Copper-Rump Humming bird is at every flower. Nearer to home, the chirpy-cheepy House Wren and the ubiquitous Bananaquit hoping to find a sugar feeder or impatiently trailing wisps of dried grass to build a seemingly impossible strategically placed home at a bough's end.

The Rain Forest is full of exemplary varieties, such as the White–tailed Sabrewing Humming Bird, the Blue-backed Manakin, the dancing birds of the forest. The Golden Olive Woodpecker, the Yellow-legged Thrush – our operatic star and that other melodious songster, the White Throated Thrush. Overhead the Orange-winged Parrot, iridescent green.

We have a variety of Raptors: The Great Black Hawk over the forest, often the Broad-Winged. Near the sea the Osprey; between the coconuts, the high speed Merlin; the Yellow-headed Caracara and Peregrine Falcon.

There are many other species of gorgeous Humming Bird such as the White-necked Jacobin, the Ruby-topaz, the Black-throated Mango, the Rufous-breasted Hermit, and the Blue-chinned Sapphire amongst others.

At Little Tobago Bird Sanctuary the most delightful, the Blue Crowned Mot Mot and Tobago's superstar the Red-billed Tropic Bird. Then there are the wetland birds. Most common are the Cattle Egret, the Little Egret, the stately Great Egret, the Snowy Egret, the Black-Bellied Tree Duck, the White-cheeked Pintail, the Anhinga, looking like a flying javelin, the Grebes, the Least and the Pied, tiny birds that dive, the Gallinules, the common and the Purple, the Little Blue Heron and the Green-backed. Come to Tobago for a banquet of birds, they are right there, even in your hotel grounds – *in fact, right outside your window.*

See over, Birds of Tobago – A beautiful poster illustrating many of the islands's more common feathered inhabitants.

SCULPTURES IN GREEN

The unique, bizarre shapes of plants known as succulents are the result of adaptations which allow these plants to withstand long periods of drought. Fleshy leaves, stems and roots act as water storage tanks and characterize all succulents including cactus plants. 'The barrel' of the stem collects water, while the spikes (modified leaves) ward off thirsty animals. Evaporation is reduced and limited through the shade provided by its natural shape and the thick waxy surface minimizes water loss. The Prickly Pear cactus' seeds were dried and ground into flour by Native American Indians while the edible paddles are today sold in supermarkets in the U.S.A. for use in Salsa preparation.

The most common local usage for the cactus variety found in many backyards in Tobago is as a natural shampoo due to its soapy qualities when peeled and lathered.

Birds of Tobago

1. Magnificent Frigatebird
2. Fish Hawk
3. Yellow-crowned Night Heron
4. Great Blue Heron
5. Rufescent Tiger-Heron
6. Short-tailed Swift
7. Red-billed Tropicbird
8. Laughing Gull
9. Brown Pelican
10. Great Egret
11. Southern Lapwing
12. Green-backed Heron
13. White-tipped Dove
14. Ruddy Ground-Dove
15. White-tailed Nightjar
16. Red-crowned Woodpecker
17. Cocoa Woodcreeper
18. Shiny Cowbird
19. Crested Oropendola
20. Carib Grackle
21. Rufous-tailed Jacamar
22. Orange-winged Parrot
23. Green-rumped Parrotlet
24. Ruby-topaz hummingbird(M)
25. Rufous-breasted Hermit
26. Copper-rumped Hummingbird
27. Black-throated Mango
28. Bare-eyed Thrush
29. Smooth-billed Ani
30. Blue-crowned Motmot
31. Tropical Mockingbird
32. House Wren
33. Sooty Grassquit
34. Tropical Kingbird
35. Yellow-bellied Elaenia
36. Barred Antshrike (M)(F)
37. Bananaquit
38. Blue-gray Tanager
39. Palm Tanager
40. Rufous-vented Chachalaca
41. White-lined Tanager (M) (F)

Poster by Sonia Canals. On sale islandwide.

HEAVEN FOR BIRD WATCHERS
CUFFIE RIVER NATURE RETREAT

On the edge of Tobago's Rain forest, surrounded by ancient trees, bamboo groves and lush vegetation, the Nature Retreat and Eco-Lodge lies gently cradled in the Runnemede Valley – a secluded yet modern facility set against a backdrop of hills. It's encircled by cool fresh-water springs and pools - a veritable oasis of calm and serenity set in an ocean of greenery, perfect for naturalists and bird lovers. According to a recent bird census, the place offers the ultimate in bird watching with its 98 species; Tanagers and Bananaquits were feeding on a table of fruit just feet away, while a couple of stunning Mot-Mots looked on in their quiet unconcerned way. Walking in through the trails, we encountered no end of Fly Catchers, elusive Manakins, Humming Birds, Woodpeckers and Tree Creepers that followed us up the path - truly a bird watchers paradise.

Male Barred Antshrike

Celebrating a wedding, anniversary or honeymoon? The retreat offers several Togetherness Packages and there is a special if you have attained your Golden Anniversary. However, you don't have to be a resident of the Lodge to savour its delights. Enjoy a 3-hour stroll or hit the trails for a full days hike, or just come and have an excellent lunch in the company of nature's bounteous beauty.

Go on, spoil yourself ....for the rest of your life!!
www.cuffieriver.com

Strictly For The Birds
The Mystery Of Migration

By David Rooks

The theory is that the migration of birds from the Northern regions to Central & South America has to do with returning 'home' when desirable & nutritious food is prevalent, and going North in summer has to do with less predators being around when there are chicks in the nest. They spend a longer time in their warm habitats than in the colder climates. Some of the birds start arriving in late August and leave in late March to the end of April.

However, this not the whole truth because a few of our migrants come from the South, such as the Fork-tailed Fly Catcher. Several others are occasional visitors from other directions, as in the 80's & 90's we regularly had Scarlet & Glossy Ibis at Buccoo Marsh. Unfortunately, many types of human developments are spreading like a fungus over the tropical feeding grounds, creating starvation conditions. Like a flood out of control, shopping malls, beef farms for supplying cheap burger joints, housing developments, golf courses, car parks and such like are reducing the birds' feeding grounds. The result is that birds are going South but not returning having died of starvation from being unable to find their ancestral feeding plants with which they had evolved.

Bird migration is phenomenal; tiny birds nest all over the US & Canada as far as the tundra and flocks appear as clouds when they leave as summer is coming to an end. One weather radar operator told me they appear as fog on his screens.

The first start arriving in August; I once netted a Blue-winged Teal in early September that had a Fish & Wildlife I.D ring. Their response was that the bird was born that year and was ringed in Canada in August.

Birds navigate by many means, such as the learned experience of their elders' memorized landmarks. Using the gravitational and magnetic forces of the Earth, they sometimes go wrong when blown off-course by strong winds. On occasion birds from the tropics are found in New England and even old England, or birds from England are seen here on the rare occasion and also the permanent resettlement of Cattle Egrets from Africa.

The list of recorded migrants to Tobago is quite exhaustive and includes the Peregrine Falcon, Great Blue Heron, Laughing Gull, White Tailed Tropic Bird, Fork Tailed Fly Catcher and the American Coot.

It was a lucky day for Tobago in 1776, when after many determined years of perseverance in its cause; the forest reserve was eventually legally protected thereby making it the oldest reserve in the western world.

Fortuitously, it was realised back then that the rain forest attracted rain and that without it Tobago's water supply would be disrupted and crops would fail. The plantation owners and speculators needed land for their cash crops of cocoa, coconuts and sugarcane and would certainly have cleared the forests and sold the timber as they had done in other parts of the island. The rain forest provides other functions like controlling soil erosion and allowing clear water to flow year round into the sea, which in turn protects the beautiful reefs at Speyside, Englishman's Bay, Castara, Culloden and Buccoo.

Fishing and tourism activities are dependent on the reefs and would decline if deforestation occurred as there would be an increase in sediment and change in the saltiness of the seawater. These would impact negatively on the reef systems.

Many Tour Guides are also employed to show visitors the delights of the rain forest with its stunning wildlife, beautiful vistas and easy access.

They are called rain forests as they are tree covered areas in warm regions where rainfall averages over 200 cm per year, allowing for year round growth. *So now you know, go take a hike!*

THE RAIN FOREST

TAKE A HIKE

Info kind courtesy of Environment Tobago

Orchids

The Beauty Queens of the Flower World

More than one-half of the Earth's diverse plant species live in tropical forests. In lush, tropical environments plants compete with one another for sunlight. Vines race each other up tree-trunks to reach the sunlit canopy and air-plants (orchids and others) attach themselves to branches and compete for every inch of the precious light rays. Closer to and down at ground zero, plants employ an adaptory ruse of dark red or mottled leaves to help absorb sunlight.

Most tropical orchids grow on trees and belong to that grouping of plants that take up residence on trees and are known as epiphytes.

From the forest canopy they receive more light and better exposure to pollinators and more efficient seed dispersal than plants on the rain-forest floor.

Some special adaptations allow them to survive in environments where water and nutrients are scarce, hence the swollen barrel stems and highly absorbent spongy cell roots. While not as common as tree orchids, terrestrial orchids i.e. those that live with their roots in the soil, thrive in a range of tropical habitats from the shady moist environs of the forest floor to the mossy vertical cliffs of waterfalls which are favoured by some types of slipper orchids. Large colonies can also find a home on dry sunny expanses of rocky outcrops, sending their roots deep inside the crevices. Listen to the soundtrack of rain forest animals as you look for orchids on your rainforest walk; also tree frogs, myriad insects and the ever present trilling of squadrons of song birds. ***Explore more – enjoy more!***

Some Tobago Flowers

TOBAGO HERITAGE FESTIVAL
"SHE BECOMES MORE..."

Bago Carnival
TOBAGO FESTIVALS COMMISSION presents
A Taste of MAS & MUSIC

TOBAGO JAZZ EXPERIENCE

Chapter 4

ANNUAL
MAIN EVENTS

UP, UP AND AWAY

GO FLY A KITE!
BOXING DAY & NEW YEAR'S DAY

Kite flying in Trinidad & Tobago is a rite of passage and Tobago boys begin making kites from an early age. They are known locally as 'Mad Bulls' – due to the roaring sound they make in the air and the strength required to hold them. It's a boyhood passion in these Islands and some grow into manhood never losing the love of it. The lads from Bethel Village have won the 'Massive Kite' category for some past years and needed a truck to bring their 20-foot entry into the grounds.

FLYING COLOURS Kite Festival is the place to be; a must-see date for the perfect family day held on the playing fields next to the Mystery Tombstone. The show kicks off at 10 a.m. with the under 14's Junior Section. The rules require all contestants to hoist, display and retrieve their kites within the 5 minute time frame. There's an allocated area for free flying kites not registered in the competition, which is a lighthearted fun filled affair.

There's music, food and bars in a great all-day picnic-style setting – perhaps the best Christmas present you could give to your loved ones or to yourself. A good-humoured and capable Afro-American lady – Valerie Critten-Stewart, created the festival and it has grown into a great day out. *Go Fly yuh Kite!*

COUNTDOWN TO CARNIVAL

BMOBILE SOCA SPREE

A massive pre-carnival open air soca jam featuring the best of the Islands' Soca Artistes'.

SOCA UNDER THE SAMAAN TREE

Tobago's popular Radio Tambrin's pre-carnival jam session with local artistes and Trinidad's Soca/Calypso stars performing their latest offerings. A wonderful open air concert.

ONE OF
THE TRADITIONS OF THE
TRINIDAD CARNIVAL

Calypsonian, Hollis 'Chalkdust' Liverpool, a former History teacher and many times Calypso Monarch, researched and published an account of the massive contributions of the enslaved Africans to the traditions of Carnival in an excellent dissertation for his Ph.D entitled - Rituals of Power & Rebellion - The Carnival Tradition in T&T 1763 to 1962. Read it to fully overstand...

As the most populous group on the island, the Africans used their remembered traditions and celebratory practices to resist the attemps by the ruling elite to oppress and control them through laws, regulations and other discriminatory acts, whereby distinct changes in the Carnival occured in 1838 (after slavery's end) the 1860's, 1900 and the late 1930's and 60's.

THE STICK FIGHTERS

From the outset, bands of stick fighters accompanied by female praise singers (latter-day flag women) dancing and singing songs of pomp and authority to ward off the powers of the opponents, is one such tradition that was handed down from the time of the enslaved Africans when stick fighters from the various plantations and villages met to 'do battle' spurred on by the Kalenda rhythms, songs and dances employed in their celebrations of the Cannes Brulees (burning cane) at Carnival time.

The structure of the songs they sung form in part the basis of the latter-day road march calypso in their call and response formats. In 1868 the colonial government passed laws banning the carrying of torches, the playing of or dancing to any drum and the management of Carnival was placed in the hands of the police; but the Africans would not surrender their rights of freedom as the stick fighters persisted in their traditional arts and vowed to carry on. It all came to a head when one Captain Baker, a military man who had had his previous tour of duty in South Africa, was appointed Commandant of the Police Force and succeeded in controlling stick fighting by placing heavily armed police guards at the meeting places and in 1880 he stopped the Cannes Brulees procession and took away all the torches and sticks he could find. However, the following year saw the stick fighters and revellers join forces and prepare in earnest to battle with the police. At midnight on Carnival Sunday (Carnival was held over 3 days) as the Cathedral bell rang, the revellers blew their horns, lit their torches and began singing to the Kaldenda rhythms -

"Mooma, Mooma, Yuh son in de grave a'ready,
Mooma, Mooma, Bring a 'kerchief and band up yuh belly".

The police ambushed them at the corner of Duke and George Streets (Hell Yard) in East Port of Spain, but were forced to withdraw as running battles spread to adjoining streets. About 50 revellers were severely wounded as were 39 policemen. Fearing an escalation of the affray, the Governor confined the police to their barracks and agreed to meet the thousands of revellers at the Eastern Market at 5 pm the following day. Accompanied only by his Aide de Camp and Secretary, Governor Freeling expressed his regrets to the revellers in his own words - "I did not know you attached so much importance to

your Masquerade. You can enjoy yourselves for the 2 days and I will give you the town for your Masquerade if you promise not to make any disturbance or break the law. I shall give orders that the police shall not molest or interfere with you if you keep within the law".

One of the heroes of the 1881 riots was the leader of the stick fighters named Joe Talmana, who struck the sword carrying Captain Baker with such force that it almost dismounted the Police Chief. Many songs and chants were sung in the parades in the 1880's through the streets of Arouca, Princes Town and San Fernando which reflected the reactions to the banning of the Cannes Brulees -

"When the bayonet charge
is the Rod of Correction
Sans d'humanite (without mercy)".

Today, the art of stick fighting appears on the official Carnival Programme as a competition often held in Arima or annually in Chaguanas but it can also be witnessed in some rural towns like Moruga, Mayaro, Sangre Grande and the Cannes Brulees ritual is celebrated annually near to the place where the riots took place, Hell Yard, being the home of one of the greatest and earliest steel bands, Trinidad All Stars - a direct link with the past barrack yards where the freed former slaves lived in the City and where they practiced the Kalenda songs and chants...

"The sound of the drum, Mama Yo,
The sound of the drum in the junction".

"When I'm dead, bury mi clothes
Don't bother to cry for me..."

T&T Carnival ~
The Greatest Show on Earth

The Carnival Season begins immediately after Christmas and builds up to a climax on the Parade days.

Almost all the islands of the West Indies celebrate Carnival, but T&T are recognised as the true masters of its art forms.

The three main ingredients of this phenomenal extravaganza are: -
Calypso or **Kaiso** – the 'old school' traditional style of composing witty, sometimes naughty, often poignant lyrical refrains and **Soca** music – the hard-driving, faster, more contemporary popular hybrid. The singers (calypsonians) compete for the national titles of Calypso Monarch and Soca Monarch with Junior titles for the youngsters. The song that's played the most wins the coveted 'Road March' title.

Calypso Tents – the venues where the singers perform nightly in a Music-Hall atmosphere of laughter and gaiety.

Steel Bands play Calypsos during this festive time and provide the passion for the rhythmic excellence demonstrated on the national instrument the Steel Drum, cleverly invented on these twin islands. They all compete for the national honour of Panorama Champs.

Carnival is Colour !
Carnival is Fete !

Carnival is Fun
Eating, drinking,
dancing in the sun.
Sharing, Caring, Lovin
and Laughing at the
Amazing.

Free your mind and the
rest will follow
Wine your waist like
there's no tomorrow.
Deliver up yourself to it
Jump up high and lift
your Spirit

(dates variable
- check beforehand)

FEBRUARY

Pan Yards – Steel drums are locally called pan and the playing of them referred to as 'beating pan'. Consequently the storage and rehearsal spaces occupied by a steel band are appropriately named 'Pan Yards' by virtue of the large area needed to house the huge mobile orchestras that perform at the Panoramas and on the streets at Carnival time.

Masquerade aka Mas is the costumery ingeniously designed and built by the citizens who are transformed into characters from the world of the imagination. There's **'Ole Mas and Mud Mas** that's played at day break (J'Ouvert) and the themed **Costume Mas** that draws visitors from all over the world to see 'THE GREATEST SHOW ON EARTH'.

Mas players compete for Carnival King and Queen titles and the bands for 'Band of the Year'.

Mas Camps – Places where the costumes are made and sold. They are free, fun to visit and to soak up the atmosphere in an unobtrusive way. Buy a costume and join a band if the spirit moves you. **Go Play Yourself.............**

THE REIGN OF THE MERRY MONARCH

Carnival Queens & Kings of the Masquerade
Pomp and Majesty riding high in the parade
Calypso Lords and Dukes on the radio
Soca divas blazing on the stereo
Pan Champs rule the musical Arenas
With works of art from mystical Arrangers.

Carne – Latin for flesh/meat; **Vale** – Latin for farewell = **Carnival** – Farewell to the flesh which precedes the 40-day Lenten period when Catholics and some Christians abstain from meat and other worldly pleasures. The period is in itself a reference to Christ's 40 days of temptation in the wilderness. Lent begins on Ash Wednesday the day after Mardi Gras (Fat Tuesday) and ends on Easter Sunday, the 3rd day after Good Friday, which of course is the day on which Christ was crucified. Its origins are to be found in the ancient pagan custom of the **Saturnalia** that was modified by the Church of Rome.

www.ncctt.org

This European tradition was brought to the Islands by the Catholic French planters – hence, for example, Dimanche Gras, Sunday before the parade. Carnivals have become very much a part of West Indian culture. New Orleans and Rio Carnival in Brazil are the world's other well-known Carnivals, albeit with other genres of music and costume and parade traditions.

T&T immigrants have established Carnivals similar to their own wherever they have settled abroad in large numbers: - London's Notting Hill, Brooklyn's Labor Day, Toronto's Caribana and Mas in Miami are the majors that provide employment annually for T&T's Carnival musicians, singers/performers and costume makers.

The cities in which they are held enjoy the huge revenues that accompany the Carnivals and these in turn help to foster multi-racial and multi-cultural relations with the host communities. *Way to go T&T.........*

FEBRUARY

PAN TRINBAGO

PANORA

'Celebratin

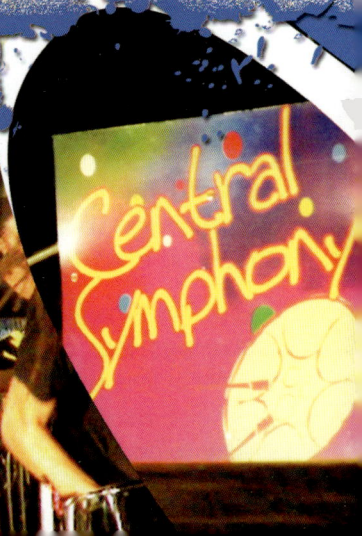

Central Symphony

AMBU HERBERT'S
RAVE.
PARD MANAGER:
ETHELBERT JA

I.A.
MA FINALS
'n Excellence'

LCB'S
Buccoo
NLCB
STEEL ORG
Chance Street, Buccoo, Tobago/Re

OUR

Petrotrin
STEEL

HOPE

Bago's Bar
CROWN POINT
J'OUVERT
2K10

CROWN POINT
J'OUVERT

OLD TIME CHARACTERS

FEBRUARY

One of the most loved art forms, full of wit and double meanings

CALYPSO, CALYPSO!

Pretty Mas, Pretty Good

tobago CARNIVAL Regatta

New improved version of one of Tobago's long time fun events, now held in the Carnival Season @ Pigeon Point; 3 days of competitive races and lots of fun and laughter with bum boats, kite boarding, windsurfers and dinghies - beautiful people on Tobago's most beautiful beach - days out for the whole family.

www.regattapromotions.com

FEBRUARY

78

BLUE MARLIN

Tobago
INTERNATIONAL
Game Fishing Tournament

Winners of Tobago Best Event Award 2011, having staged 16 consecutive Tournaments over the years in the picturesque village of Charlotteville; Sailfish, Marlins, Grouper and Tuna were among the 2010 species caught or tagged and released by 169 anglers from the U.S.A, Canada, U.K. and the Caribbean from 58 boats, bringing in 2500 pounds of fish to scale including a 264 lb Grouper.

The year 2011 saw the event team up with the Fishing Association's Marlin Madness Tournament to present the Tobago Billfish Bonanza.

TIGFT is a qualifying event for the IGFA / Bonnier International Tournament of Champions and is also a member of the Southern Caribbean Billfish Circuit. www.tgft.com

MARCH

BUCCOO GOAT RACE FESTIVALS
Running Strong & Going Good at 80+

The Goat Race Festival begun in 1925 and for many years was the major activity on the village recreation ground. Area development forced a shift of venue to the Battery and thence to its current and permanent home. The festivals are held annually at Buccoo on the Sunday after Carnival, on Easter Monday at Mount Pleasant and the premier event on Easter Tuesday, a de facto Tobago holiday at Buccoo and also during the July/August Heritage Festival.

The pioneers of goat racing have now all passed on, but their legacy in the form of the Goat Race Committee within the Village Council remains a landmark in community development through voluntary service.

Buccoo elder, Sonny Murray accompanied his dad, spending many hours in constructing the race track rails and was President of the Committee for more than 20 years. He still trains apprentice jockeys in the sport as well as keeping his eyes and senses focused to ensure continuity.

Pick your goat as they head to the starting gate; the competition's keen and the stakes are high. Come ready to have a grand time! Place your bets among your friends and family and then try your luck at winning a crab race – but practice walking sideways beforehand!

Music and laughter and foods and drinks – a must see, must do for the entire family – Touch Tobago!

IT'S GOAT RACE TIME

It's all the 'fun of the fair' at Goat Race time with its spankin' new purpose-built complex. Enjoy the races in fine style. A hilarious spectacle and first class family entertainment that's been a delight to visitors and locals alike for over 80 years.

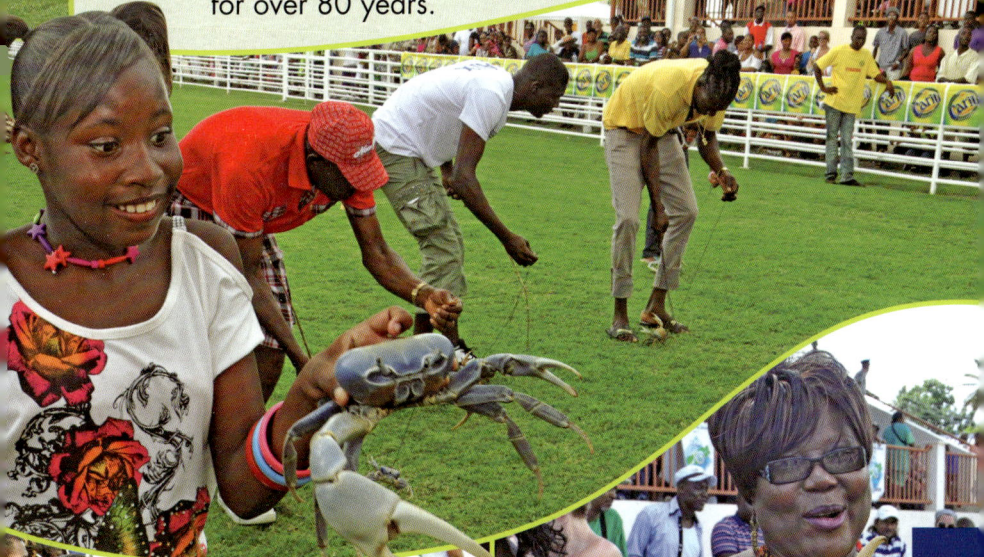

Sizzling hot performers from around the region have the audience dancing in the aisles kicking off the start of tobago jazz experience weekend

TOBAGO JAZZ EXPERIENCE 2010
APRIL 22nd to 25th

MOUNT IRVINE
BAY HOTEL &
GOLF CLUB

MT. IRVINE'S

Jazz on the beach
& Jazz belles

It gets better each year...kick back on a deck chair, walk bare foot on the sand, treat yourself to a fabulous lunch while listening to authentic jazz on mt. Irvine hotel beach – perfect days for the perfect lime...

TOBAGO JAZZ EXPERIENCE 2010
APRIL 22nd to 25th

Jazz
EXPERIENCE

Photos courtesy: Ossie Brown Tourism Div

SWEET MUSIC FOR
DAYS & DAYS...

INTERNATIONAL STARS BLESSED WITH VOICES TO TOUCH HEARTS AND ELEVATE THE LISTENERS' SPIRITS...THE BEST LOCAL TALENT PERFORMING ACROSS THE ISLAND'S TOURISM CENTRES –

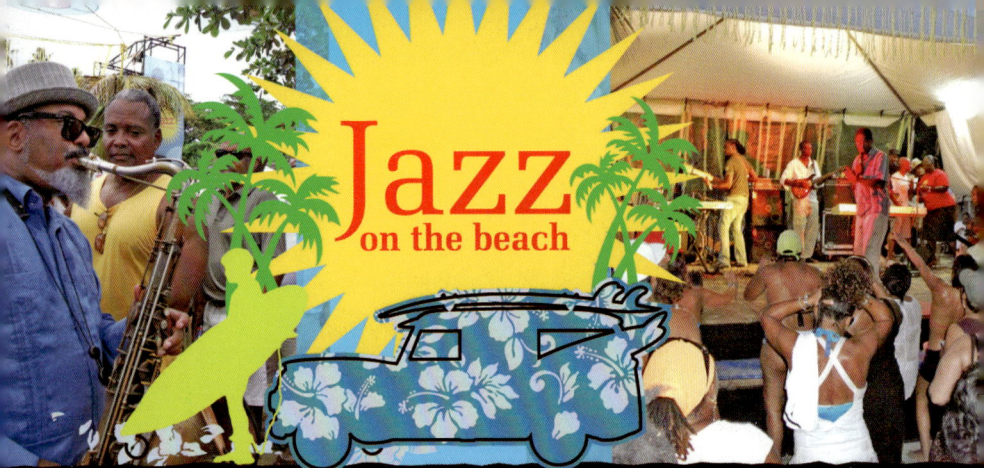

Jazz
on the beach

THE GIG THAT APPEALS TO BEACH LOVERS

– SOME OF WHOM ENJOY THE SHOW FROM THE LUXURY OF THE SOOTHING WATERS – A BEAUTIFUL LIME WITH BEAUTIFUL PEOPLE – LOVE UP!

88

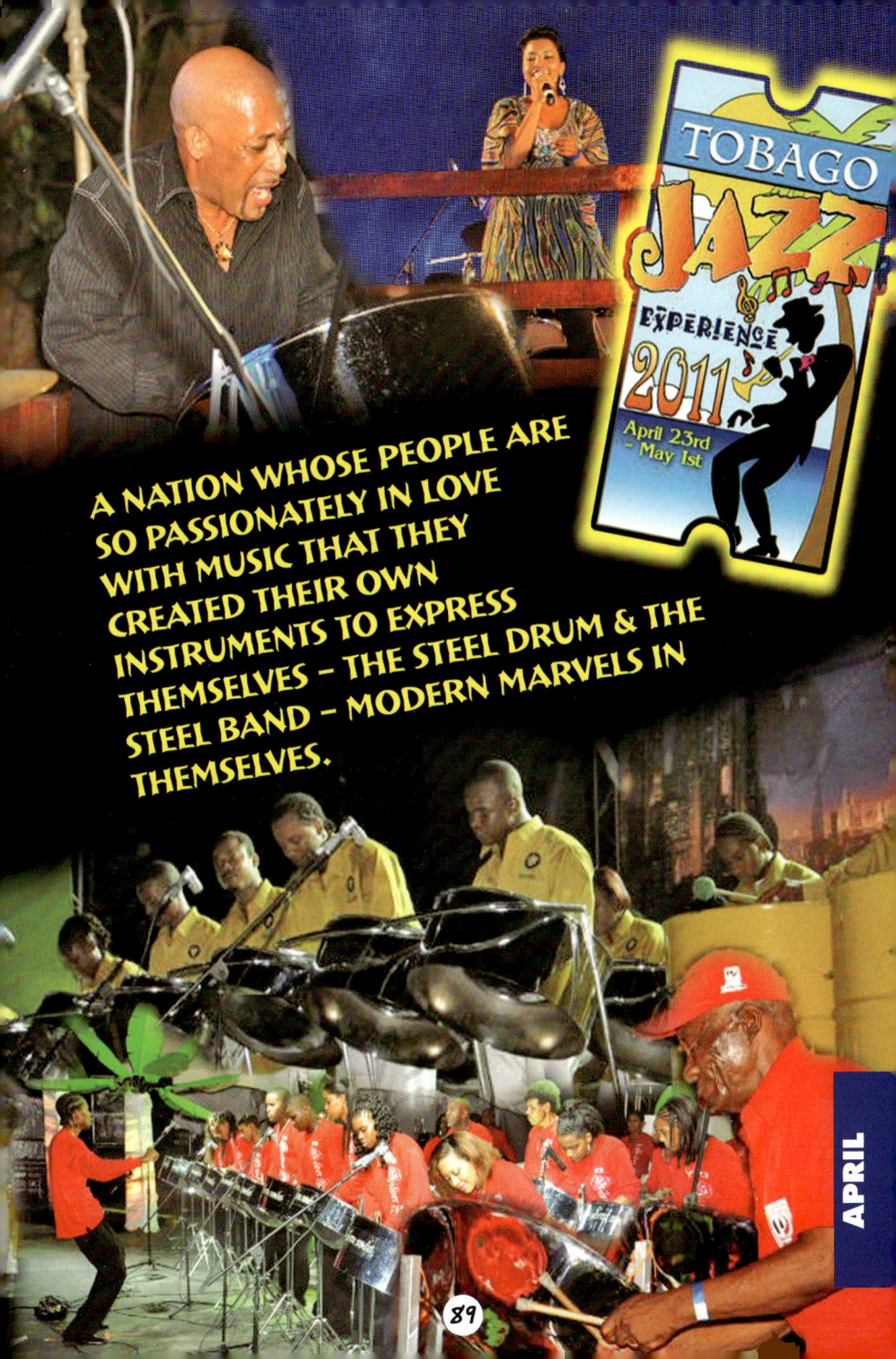

TOBAGO **JAZZ** EXPERIENCE **2011**

April 23rd
– May 1st

A NATION WHOSE PEOPLE ARE SO PASSIONATELY IN LOVE WITH MUSIC THAT THEY CREATED THEIR OWN INSTRUMENTS TO EXPRESS THEMSELVES – THE STEEL DRUM & THE STEEL BAND – MODERN MARVELS IN THEMSELVES.

cooks in competition

Yabba
I
up

Cou Cou
Tun
I
Coconut
Cou Cou

Fou Fou
I
Pound
Plantin

Lippy
Lappa

CULINARY
ARRIVE HUNGRY
AND LEAVE FULL...
FESTIVAL

THE ISLAND'S BEST
CHEFS WILL MAKE
SURE OF THAT,
PLUS MUSIC TO HELP
THE FOOD DIGEST!

MAY

Photos by
Ossie Browne
Tourism Div.

90

TOYOTA TOBAGO
RAINBOW CUP
TRIATHLON

Rainbow Warriors Triathlon on Turtle Beach has been going for the past 7 years - Swim, Bike, Run organised by Race Director Jason Gooding, Trinidad's Triathlon champ; ably assisted by club members and a wide selection of sponsors. A terrific fun event which makes a valuable contribution to Tobago's Calendar of Events.

www.rainbowtri.com

MAY

CHIEF SECRETARY'S

CHARITY GOLF TOURNAMENT

This latest golf tournament is the brainchild of sports enthusiast and amiable businessman Jeffery Azar, in recognition of the Office of the Assembly's Chief Secretary but also particularly as a tribute to the current Office Holder- the Honourable Orville London.

Dates for the Tournament change annually and these are set by T&T's Golf Association to avoid clashing with other tournaments, thereby encouraging wider participation from local and regional golfers.

DWIGHT YORKE INTERNATIONAL GOLF TOURNAMENT

Local boy made good - Manchester United's football hero has his sporting friends, among other stars from the entertainment world in his own golfing tournament.
www.visittobago.gov.tt

JUNE

CHARLOTTEVILLE FISHERMEN'S FEST

Fishermen celebrate on their special day with St. Peter, the original fisher of men in mind. Lots of food, drinks and water sports; with all day music and live tamboo bamboo from the village drummers. A great day out to enjoy rural Tobago at its very best.

TOBAGO HERITAGE FESTIVAL

"SHE BECOMES MORE BEAUTIFUL"

She Becomes more Beautiful

The Tobago Heritage Festival which began in 1987 is an island wide event, the like of which you would certainly not experience anywhere else in the world. This fact has its basis in the celebrations of the African cultural heritage unique to the inhabitants of this island. At this time, more than any other time of the year, the Tobago population is bound together by their shared past and kinship.

Village Councils are drawn from within various villages in Tobago to organize, produce and host musical and dramatic contributions to the festival. Some villages have become associated with specific themes and therefore stage the same annual production, albeit with various cast and costume changes. Moriah's 'Old Time Tobago Wedding' complete with ceremony, procession and reception, is a good example; also Pembroke's 'Salaka Feast', which involves rites, rituals and mass cook-outs in

JULY

cont'd over

the morning and afternoon and a spectacular stage production at night. The villagers bake whole pigs in the earth and the feast is enjoyed by everyone.

Every aspect of the cultural heritage of the islanders is highlighted and explored – from domestic chores of days-gone-by to children's games, Christmas customs and funeral rites. Fishermen's shanties and celebratory jigs and reels, folk tales and superstitions to rites of passage; Tobago folk pull out all the stops and celebrate life – past and present.

If you are fortunate enough to be in Tobago at this time, get yourself along to one or several of these casual but dignified affairs that are held open-air.

Be prepared to be surprised by the range of the productions and the keen, joyful participation of the villagers. *For once in your life!*

Festival Office - 639-4441

JULY

TOBAGO HERITAGE FESTIVAL

"SHE BECOMES MORE BEAUTIFUL"

TOBAGO HERITAGE FESTIVAL — MORE BEAUTIFUL THAN EVER...
AN ISLANDWIDE PREMIER CULTURAL EXPERIENCE
A SUPERLATIVE AFFAIR...BE AMAZED, BE DELIGHTED

UNDERWATER CARNIVAL

A week of great diving, seminars and fun for all diving levels at the best dive sites around Tobago. See the website *www.tobagounderwatercarnival.com* for information.

JULY

GREAT FETE WEEKEND

The Great Fete Weekend is a huge annual beach party at Pigeon Point beach. Top DJ's. Soca & Dancehall stars from T&T & Jamaica make this an unmissable NO.1 Beach Party in the Southern Caribbean.

Tobago

WEST INDIES

CARIBBEAN SEA

SIST

PARLATU

ENGLISHMANS BAY

CASTARA BAY

KING PETERS BAY

CULLODEN BAY

ARNOS VALE BAY

PLYMOUTH

Gt COURLAND BAY

MORIAH

FORT BENNETT

STONE HAVEN BAY

MASON HALL

PIGEON POINT

Mt IRVINE BAY

FORT GEORGE

BUCCOO BAY

BUCCOO REEF

BLACK ROCK

CARNBEE

BA

HILLSBOROUG

BACOLET BAY

LAMBEAU

SCARBOROUGH

STORE BAY

LITTLE ROCKLY BAY

FORT MILFORD

CROWN POINT INT. AIRPORT

CANOE BAY

KS 🐚

ST GILES ISLANDS 🐚

MAN O' WAR BAY ☀️🐚

PIRATES BAY ☀️🐚

L'ANSE FOURMI ☀️🐚

FLAGSTAFF HILL 🌺

BLOODY BAY ☀️🐚

SHOPS

CHARLOTTEVILLE ☀️🍶🐚

LITTLE TOBAGO ☀️🐚

RAINFOREST RESERVE

SPEYSIDE ☀️🍶🐚🌺

ARGYLE FALLS 🌺

DELAFORD 🍶🌺

RICHMOND GREAT HOUSE 𝕳

ROXBOROUGH 🍶 Ⓟ

KINGS BAY ☀️

OROUGH DAM 🌺

QUEENS BAY 🌺

BELLE GARDEN 🍶𝕳

PRINCES BAY ☀️

GLAMORGAN

CARAPUSE BAY

PEMBROKE

RICHMOND ISLAND

GOLDSBOROUGH BAY

GOODWOOD 🍶

SMITHS ISLAND

Y

FORT GRANBY ☀️🍶𝕳

LEGEND

☀️ BATHING BEACHES

🍶 FOOD AND DRINK

🐚 SNORKEL / DIVING

💲 SHOPS

𝕳 HISTORICAL SITES

🌺 BEAUTY SPOTS

Ⓟ GAS STATIONS

ATLANTIC OCEAN

©PHIL DOBSON   magicpen@tstt.net.tt

THE CARIB
GREAT RACE
How Time Flies

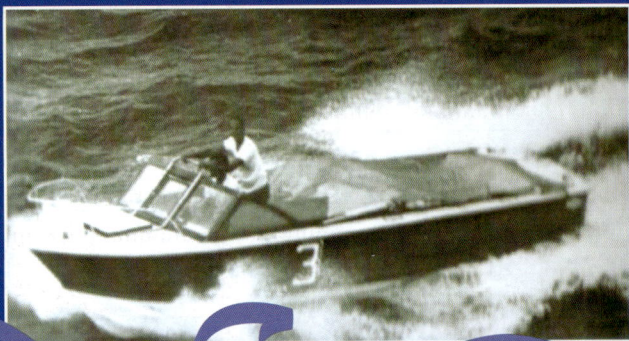

On Discovery Day, August 1, 1969, the Great Race began off Carenage in Trinidad with 62 boats participating. The winner was the 21-foot wooden Camena which narrowly beat Tranquilizer in a time of 2 hours 38 minutes.

In 2005, the legendary 14 time winner, Mr. Solo, set a course record of 58 minutes.

In 2001 Carib, Trinbago's giant brewery and long-time sponsor of numerous social and sporting events, signed a ten-year contract as the sponsor of the Great Race and has significantly increased media coverage and public awareness of the events.

Prizes are awarded to the first boat past the post in each class category. The first 10 boats to finish receive cash prizes – first prize being TT$100,000.

It's a thrilling event, broadcast live on radio and hyped up beforehand in Trinidad with a massive main street parade of the boats complete with gorgeous bikini-clad girlettes.

It's become a tradition to Tobago folk to herald the arrival of the boats with a huge all-day fete where the race ends. **Be there to cheer!**

AUGUST

T&T FILM FESTIVAL

Welcome to the T&T Film Festival, a non-profit making organisation run by a small, dedicated team of Directors supported by professionals, advisors and volunteers. Films from India and London's Black Film makers' group are among those from all over the world, while highlighting Caribbean productions.

So, if you are here at Film Festival time, go on the website below to enjoy the T&T premiere of some critically acclaimed films.

www.trinidadandtobagofilmfestival.com

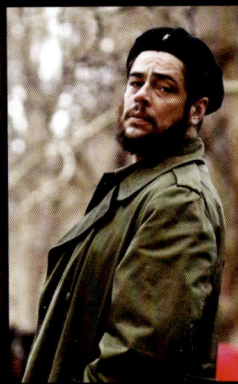

SEPTEMBER

bago

Blue Food Festival

200

ood • We **estival...** **ALL FOR FREE**

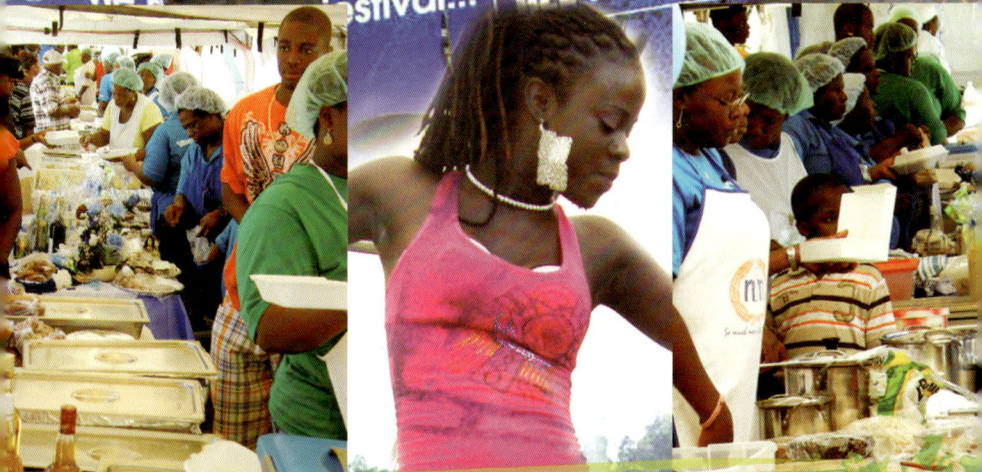

TATTOO

YARDIE

OCTOBER

105

INTERNATIONAL
CYCLING
CLASSIC

The annual battle of will, skill and stamina held on the scenic, hilly terrain of the Island has a history that goes back to 1986 when the races began. Participation has steadily increased by some of the world's top cycling teams.

It is therefore quite possible dear visitor, that you might have your own heroes from your part of the world to cheer on and maybe have your photo taken with for memories' sake.

Enjoy the Lime!!

Chapter 5
MUSIC
& ARTS

TOBAGO DRUMMERS

from the Cradle ---- to the Grave ....

The people of Tobago have a great love for the traditional folk arts of dance and song, which are accompanied by the hard-driving West African rhythms, that are part of their heritage. These arts are fostered in the schools and at community events and are an integral part of the Island's cycle of life – from the cradle to the grave.

The Island has some renowned drummers who usually lead their groups, arranging the sequences and furthering precision and percussive skills. Hiram Scott, Dominique Williams and Wayne Guerra are a few of the Island's master drummers who contribute to the continuance of these traditions. The Culture Department, across from S'boro's market square provides events throughout the Island for them to perform publicly.

Try to see them perform at hotels or festivals and put your finger on the pulse of Tobago.

If you are a player or collector, there are a trio of drum-making outlets at Fort Bennett, Arnos Vale and Wayne Guerra's home, next to WASA at Lowlands.

Go www.whatsonintobago.com for the Island's Calendar of Events.

TAMBRIN MUSIC

These drums, similar in design to tambourine drums, are indigenous instruments to Tobago – in as much the same way that steel drums are the creation of the people of Trinidad.

The Tobago folks came up with the idea of covering old circular cheese boxes with goat skin to create a more subdued sounding instrument that would be accompanied by a tinkling triangle and strident fiddle to produce the reels and jigs that constitute that unique art form that has become known as Tambrin music.

Nowadays, the bands, usually five in number (3 drums plus fiddle and triangle), use the wood of the easily-bent wild cassava plant to make the drum frames and small fires are required to heat the drum skins just prior to performances.

In Tobago there are several Tambrin Bands in existence whose music can be enjoyed at cultural events. The Island's Culture Department has become increasingly aware of the need to pass on this unique Tobago tradition via the schools and community education programmes.
Drag yuh bow Mr. Fiddler!

CARIBBEAN CARVERS

In the African Tradition -
Tobago Style

Blessed with an abundant variety of woods to create their masterpieces and using handmade adaptations as the tools of their trade, these artisans display degrees of skill and concepts that seem to hark back to their African roots and the love for this particular art-form.

Visit any of these sun-kissed islands and one will find bountiful examples of Caribbean carving.

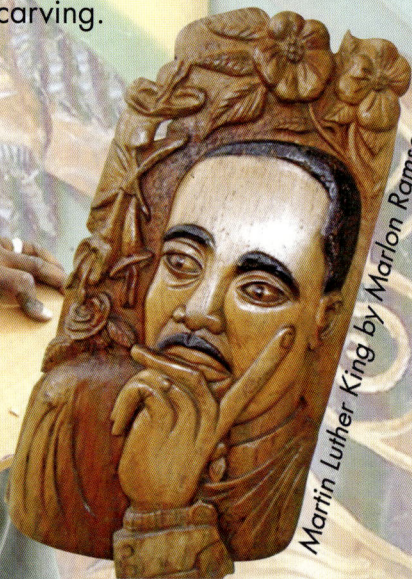

Martin Luther King by Marlon Ramsey

Usually unschooled in the typical art college's methodology, the average carver works to produce items for the tourism market. Get yourself an original – a memento that will be yours, for your own lifetime and beyond.

The numerous souvenir shops around the island and Store Bay's Craft Market all stock works by these master carvers and in fact there is a new pocket directory of this island's artisans with all their contact details that is now available free of charge from the usual outlets - courtesy of the World Travel Foundation with an eye on sustainability of the tourism industry.

Tobago Music Makers

Tobago's Visual Artists

Luise Kimme

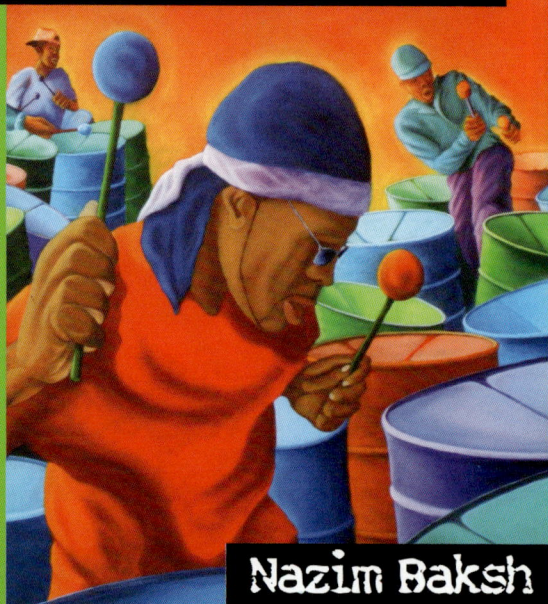

Nazim Baksh

Dillon's Bamboo Paintings

The Art Gallery

Original Paintings
Limited Edition Prints
Portraiture
Art Exhibitions
Framing
Photography
Art & Interior Consultants

HORIZONS
FRAMING & DECOR LTD.

Kartik
HOME DECOR

Shore Things
Café & Craft

Store Bay's
ARTS AND CRAFTS

THINGS NATURAL

DRUMMERS OF TOMORROW

PASSING ON THE TRADITION...

Drummers of Tomorrow is one of the most dynamic groups on the Island and was founded in 1995 by a young man named Courtney Potts, whose passion is drums – the making and playing of them. Luckily for him, his older brother Freddy was involved in the annual Folk Arts Festival, so he didn't have to look far for support and inspiration.

Together with his other siblings and cousins they combined their talents and skills to create and develop their unique style of drumming. He makes his own drums from mango wood and young Courtney has been passing on the traditions by encouraging and incorporating the neighbourhood youths into the group. They've been receiving various accolades since 2001 and have successfully appeared at the World Talent competition held in Hollywood.

CALYPSO, CALYPSO T&T MUSIC

A generation before Bob Marley globalised Jamaican Reggae, Harry Belafonte had popularized the Calypso beat and music of the Caribbean by recording and performing some classic songs that have become the theme songs with which these islands are automatically associated.

'Day-O' (Daylight come, and me wan' go home) is over 50 years old and is celebrated in stadiums all over America by home-town fans who use it as their cheer song.

'Jamaica Farewell ' (Down the way, where the nights are gay) is another beautiful classic that tourists delight in hearing and singing along to when they visit the Caribbean, together with that other wonderful oldie 'Island in the Sun'.

It's perfectly natural for people worldwide to associate the singer Harry Belafonte with these classics as his first record – Calypso – was the very first album to sell more than one million copies when it was released in 1956-7, remaining at No. 1 on the Billboard Charts for a staggering 32 weeks.

Irving Burgie, aka Lord Burgess is the composer of the above titles, having written some 34 songs for Belafonte. But Belafone also worked for years on his stage shows with Trinidad's Lord Melody - singing his hit "Mama, look a boo-boo dey". Great classics like -

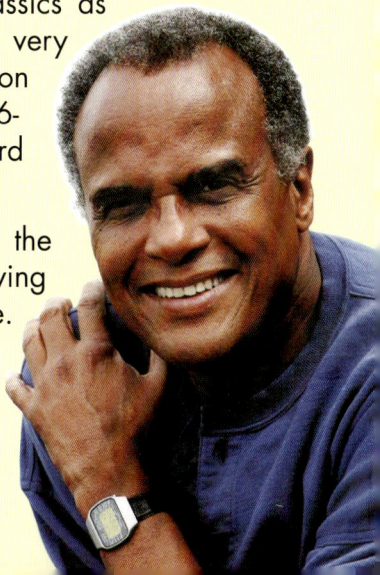

'Rum & Coca-Cola", a world-wide hit from the Andrews' Sisters, "Shame & Scandal in the Family", "Matilda", the double entendre "Big Bamboo", and "Dr. Kitch" were all composed by past masters like Lord Invader, Roaring Lion, Growling Tiger, Lord Kitchener and a host of T&T's earliest Hall of Famers.

Rock & Roll supplanted the crooners in the 50's and for today's generation Soca and Rapso have gained in popularity over the more lyrical calypso.

However, the art of calypso and ex-tempo will always remain paramount in the hearts and minds of the people in T&T as a lasting legacy of the voices of the people.

Hear them in the Calypso Tents over the Carnival Season and see them on stage in their finest hour at Dimanche Gras as they vie for the peoples' blessings to be the Calypso Monarch of T&T...*No easy feat that!*

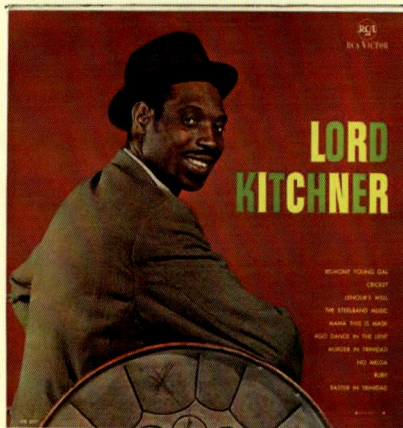

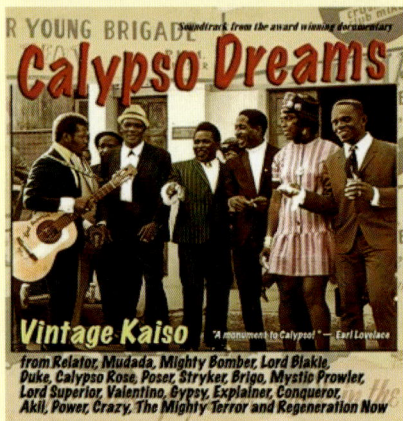

TOBAGO
History

In The Beginning .... Poison Arrows

THE CARIB EMPIRE

Every year their war-canoes would head south and gather in Tobago before going off on raids to Trinidad and the Amazonian mainland from whence they had originated. Tobago was the southernmost frontier of the Carib empire that stretched north throughout the islands. Its indigenous Amerindian population was quite small in comparison to those in Trinidad, St. Vincent and Dominica, where large communities still exist and pursue their ancient crafts and traditions.

A Spanish governor of Trinidad at that time wrote back to Spain complaining that the surrounding seas *were infested with war-like Caribs who ate their captives and carried off the women and children of the unfortunate peaceful Arawaks. They declined to eat European flesh, but took them as slaves nevertheless.*

The Caribs lived by the sea on the western part of the island and Canoe Bay is a major archeological site where numerous artifacts have been found. The Arawaks lived on the hills in the eastern part of the island.

The Manchineel trees, the roots of which prevent soil erosion and are found on some beaches, provided the poison for their arrows. Today, the Environment

Dept. displays signs at beaches where they grow, warning visitors to beware of these deadly trees, all parts of which are highly toxic. The small fruit resembles a crab-apple and one should not stand beneath these trees to shelter from the rain as the dripping water will severely burn the skin and could do serious damage to your eyes. ***BE WARNED!***

The Caribs made dugout canoes and traversed the seas in these. They slept in hammocks, made earthenware pots and kept tame parrots, pigs and pet monkeys around their thatched homes. The men hunted and fished, while the women wove baskets, tended the cassava and sweet potato crops and prepared meals for the family or preserved the fish catch by sun-drying or smoking.

A small Carib community, led by their Chief, King Cardinal lived in the Studley Park area, while King Peters Bay is another reference to their existence. They never came to peaceful terms with their would-be enslavers.

Tobago's original name was Tabaco - the long stemmed pipe which the Indians loved to smoke. Visit the interesting museum at Fort King George to go back in time and see relics of their existence.

The locals you will meet on your daily travels or at work in the hotels of Tobago are descendants of the West African peoples brought to the island to work on the sugar plantations. ***But that's another story...........................***

What's in a Name?

On his 3rd voyage, half a dozen years after his first land-fall in the Caribbean, Cristobal Colon aka Christopher Columbus came upon Trinidad, originally named Kairi or Iere. He came via the Gran Boca. Entry to Trinidad's Gulf of Paria is guarded by the Dragon's Mouth – hence Bocas – Spanish for mouth. The Bocas/Channels are 3 in number – treacherous and difficult waters for small craft and large ships that lack speed and manoeuverability.

A fortnight later he set a north-eastern course and sighted two islands – to the east Tobago and to the north Grenada. He named them Assumption and Conception respectively. Explorers like Vespucci and others who followed in his footsteps, used charts where the very same islands were referred to as Madalena and Mayo. Naturally the people they met on these islands had their own names for their island homes – they called Tobago…Tabaco or Tavaco.

All lands "discovered" by Columbus were claimed by Spain's monarchy – the expeditions' financiers who lost no time in establishing a vast domain in this New World. The riches found, plundered, taken or bartered for trinkets attracted the jealousy and attention of the other naval powers as well as privateers and buccaneers – pirates by any other name.

The Spanish and Portuguese galleons, laden with booty and bounty, became fair game to all. The "Spanish Main" became by-words for untold treasures and fortunes to do battle for.

Many of the Caribbean islands have place-names or historical sites where pirates established secluded hideouts.

THE ONSET OF THE ATLANTIC SLAVE TRADE

Prince Enrique of Portugal, 'The Navigator' dispatched his Captains to look for gold. They found slaves, an already well known but very expensive commodity in Europe.

In 1441, a Portugese sailor Antum Gonzales seized 'two moors' and took them back to Lisbon and gave them to Pope Pius II. The Pope, in turn, granted Prince Enrique title to all lands discovered East of Capo Blanco and in 1455, he authorised Portugal 'to reduce to servitude all infidel people'. Pope Pius II also directed that baptised Africans should not be traded, but they could be enslaved.

Malachi Postlethway - 18th Century Capitalist Theoretician
"The African Trade is the first principle and foundation of all the rest; the main spring of the machine that set every wheel in motion...
The African Trade is so beneficial to Great Britain, so essentially necessary to the very being of her Colonies, that without it neither could we flourish nor they long subsist".

GREED - became the primary motive of the Atlantic slave trade that lasted over 400 years.

SOME FACTS :-
The slave trade became the largest employer in Holland & Portugal from 1500 - 1750.

Barclays Bank founders, David & Alexander Barclay established their bank with profits from their slaving business.

Insurance giants, Lloyds of London became one of the biggest financial forces by dabbling in and insuring slave ships and their cargoes.

SLAVERY & SUGAR CANE

The Sugar Cane plant, native to Asia, was introduced to the Americas by Christopher Columbus; Dutch traders introduced cultivation. Its impact was revolutionary and small tobacco and cotton holdings gave way to large plantations. Many displaced colonists emigrated to the American colonies or became buccaneers.

The British set up sugar plantations bringing over African slaves to work them. The first cargo of sugar destined for England sailed in 1770. In 1780 there were over 10,500 slaves working on the Island. The remains of a sugar plantation with the water wheel and iron workings can be seen at Arnos Vale. Slavery was abolished in 1807 and because of the amount of African Slaves brought over between 1763 – 1807, Tobago became an African society ruled over by British landowners and officials. The Tobago museum at Fort George above Scarborough contains excellent examples of Amerindian artifacts, slavery items and historical information.

African slaves were separated from family, kin and tribe and strict regulations were enforced against their assembly and cultural practices e.g. Language & Drumming. Resistance to slavery took many forms including suicide, arson, escape and insurrection.

LA MAGDALENA
THE STORY OF TOBAGO 1498-1898

By David Phillips

The above named title, a most excellent history of Tobago, provides the reader with riveting details of the discovery and colonization of the island, together with the various Acts and machinations necessary to administrate this unique and beautiful colony. The author David Phillips, now deceased, worked in Colonial Banking in the Caribbean and Tobago in particular and began researching the island's history in 1975. Chairman of The Tobago Trust (creators of the Tobago Museum), he lived in retirement on the island he loved. His family runs the successful business Island Investments, from whom this excellent tome of 400 pages can be obtained.

For a factual account of the owners of the plantations and the numbers of their slaves, the various governors, accounts of the wars, skirmishes, and the politics behind the numerous decisions taken by the plantocracy and the Crown, the formation of the Assembly and the Parliamentary and governing bodies, details of yearly productions and several visitors' accounts, David Phillips has left the lovers of history a masterpiece of good writing and historical data.

A collector of antique charts of the island and books related to the history of the Caribbean, he has provided us with a thorough understanding of the history of the place names you'll encounter as you traverse the island and much, much more besides!

Explore more, Enjoy more!

Published by www.iuniverse.com.
Avl. from Island Investments, Shirvan Rd.

DUTCH FORT
BY THE SCARBOROUGH PORT

Looking out to sea from the Port, one can quite easily imagine the French Fleet attacking the Dutch Fort opposite (see the road that inclines uphill, next to Phyllis' Café) and which still bears that very name, Dutch Fort.

The Dutch settlers called the Bay, Red Rock Bay; note the cluster of rocks smack-dab in the centre of the bay, which in time evolved into Rockley Bay.

The little hill at Dutch Fort overlooks the harbour and was the natural location for any military base. This was back in 1677 when cannons had the last word so everyone built forts as attacks could come at any time including those by roaming pirates.

The Dutch safeguarded their assets by storing all their jewellery, money and female slaves on a provision ship which would sail to safety when battle commenced. Unfortunately, the treasure ship caught fire and sank in the bay along with warships from both sides. The French changed their tactics when they returned for Round Two and bombarded the Fort with red-hot fire balls. One landed in the ammunition storeroom killing most of the Dutch and giving the French possession of the island.

The bronze cannon at the Port was discovered in 1990 when dredging the harbour. It came from the French Commander of the Fleet's ship, which was lost at that very battle.

I wonder if the treasure ship was ever found, or is it still lying out there on the bottom of the bay?

Historical Tobago – Explore More. Enjoy More!!

THE RAVAGING OF TRINIDAD IN 1677
THE BUCCANEERS' REVENGE

In 1673, a buccaneer fleet set out from their base in Tortuga to sack Puerto Rico, but a hurricane caught their fleet off the coast and they were captured by the Spaniards who, of course, owned that island and many others in the Caribbean as well as various territories in the Americas. They were forced to face the full fury of the Spaniards and some were used as live targets for their bowmen and lancers. The survivors were sent to Cuba to work as forced labourers.

Eventually, the Spaniards realised that keeping such a large group prisoner, might attract a resuce mission by other buccaneers, so they shipped them off in small batches to Cadiz in Spain. Having no valid reason to hold them the Spanish deported them back to France. Being societies outcasts with no future anywhere, they caught ships back to otheir spiritual home in Tortuga where their hatred for the Spaniards festered and grew.

In March 1677, when the main French fleet attacked Tobago and the great naval battle against the Dutch was underway, a French Marquis, in command of a frigate encouraged these buccaneers to follow him and take their revenge by sacking the Spaniards in Trinidad. The frigate distracted the Spaniards and Port of Spain (Puerto Espana) was quickly taken by the buccaneers, who then swept up the Caroni river and took St. Joseph (San Jose de Oruna) completely by surprise.

The Spanish garrison had been raided so many times, that they had taken to hiding their valuables in the high woods; so the buccaneers settled down in the town for a month of mayhem sacking and raping their time away. At the end of the month they took 100,000 gold coins before setting fire to the town.

Their thirst for revenge not quite satisfied, they went on to do the same to Caracas in Venezuela before retiring, laden with booty to Tortuga.

Tobago History
Some Do's & Dont's Of ......
The Tobago Slave Act Of 1768

The Preamble – *The plantations and estates in the island cannot be managed and improved without the labour of a great number of slaves, but that these are of "Barbarous, wild and savage Natures". This necessitates laws for keeping order among them and for keeping them under subjugation. All of which will be conducive to the Security, Peace and Happiness of the Colony.*

Clause (1) That slaves maiming, wounding or striking white persons on any pretence whatsoever, except in defense of their owners' or employers' personal goods, shall suffer death or punishment proportionate to the crime. A Justice of the Peace shall be empowered to order a public whipping to any slave who insults, abuses, threatens or acts contemptuously towards a white person.

Clause (2) That slaves willfully setting fires to canes, works, dwelling houses or other buildings or who have attempted to give poison to any person, shall be put to death as felons.

Clause (8) Any slave attempting to leave the island or inveigling others to do so, shall suffer death.

Clause (19) That because of the danger inherent in slaves from different plantations banding together – "any owner letting slaves beat any drum, empty casks, great gourds or blow horns and shells, or allowing slaves belonging elsewhere to mix with their own, shall forfeit 10 pounds."

Kind courtesy – La Magdalena by David Phillips –
Available Island Investments 639-9901

The Belmanna Riots of 1876

Address by the Honourable Mr. Abbott to the House of Legislative Assembly - Thursday 11th May 1876.

Whilst executing the process of Law, a spirit of determined hostility appears to have taken possession of the people and exhibited itself in the stoning and other ill treatment of the Police...on the 5th arrest being made matters assumed a worse aspect. The Corporal (Belmanna) was thrown down more than once by the missiles aimed at him. The people became more violent and in a most unfortunate moment, it appears to have been considered necessary by the Corporal to fire in self defence. The result of this firing, which no one deplores more than I do, was the death of a woman named Mary Jane Thomas.

From this moment, riot appears to have reigned supreme - the Manager's house was gutted and the mob surrounded the Court House armed with cutlasses, sticks and other missiles. The release of the prisoners was demanded and acceded to but, this had no effect in pacifying the rioters.

The Police generally were beaten severely, but Corporal Belmanna, whose life they were determined to take most brutally so much so that he died from the wounds inflicted on him.

The day after His Excellency's arrival at Roxborough, no less than 135 persons were sworn as Special Constables, but I regret to say that since then, several of these Constables have been arrested for being involved in the disgraceful riots!!

cont'd over

THE THREE QUEENS OF THE VIRGIN ISLANDS

In 1878 three former slave ladies on St. Croix led an insurrection against the Danish government for improved working and living conditions. During this action a major portion of Frederiksted was destroyed by fire. This revolt is known today as "FIREBURN" and the ladies are renowned as "Queen Mary, Queen Agnes and Queen Matilda" – The Three Queens of the Virgin Islands.

"Through everything I have read of slaves in the Caribbean, there runs a constant thread of small but courageous acts of defiance. A spirit that would see them endure and ultimately thrive. Just look at what these people created...

These are people who, from their tiny islands, have made a mark on the world".

Andrea Levy - Writer. Winner of the Walter Scott Prize for Historical Fiction 2011

A Proclamation by Lt. Gov. R.W. Harley

Extract from the Tobago Gazette – Friday May 12th 1876

Whereas certain Acts of Incendiarism having taken place in the Windward District of this Island and great resistance having been offered to the arrest of the alleged incendiaries.............................
And whereas a certain police officer has been killed and others have been dangerously wounded in endeavouring to execute the Warrants for the arrest of the said incendiaries and whereas many persons in the said District have been guilty of serious breaches of the Peace and have used and are still using threats towards the property and persons of Her Majesty's well disposed subjects........................

I DO HEREBY DESIRE IT TO BE MADE KNOWN TO ALL - Persons who have been guilty of the said acts and also of any breach of the Peace will be speedily punished with the utmost severity of the law.

Subsequently, forty persons were indicted for murder with 16 of them being sentenced to death, later commuted to penal servitude except 2 who were later reprieved. (Slaves were expensive assets).

Some historians say that the main body of the revolt was Barbadian immigrant labourers employed on Roxborough estate, while others claim the overseers were Barbadian and harsh disciplinarians. One thing that's certain is the leader, a black woman known as 'Ti Piggi' led the protest and was shot dead by Corporal Belmanna, which act resulted in his own death by the protestors.

Courtesy La Magdalena by David Phillips

BACK-IN-TIME-TOBAGO

ORAL HISTORY

BELLE GARDEN - was known as the land of beautiful African women (still is, I guess!) It derives its name from the true story of Belle, the beautiful daughter of a rich French planter. She had created a lovely garden, which was an attraction to all travellers who either walked or rode horse carts and donkeys at that time. Part of the Richmond River became known as Belle River and the little bay where the fishing boats are is called Belle View Bay.

A wonderful aspect of this period piece is the continuation of a tradition whereby there's always someone in the village who carries the name of Belle - even today!

GOODWOOD – is the hometown of Jan Dick Babalau, a rebel runaway slave who led a rebellion against their slave masters. He was eventually caught on the grounds, which today are at the entrance to the Community Centre, hanged from a fiddlewood tree and buried in Nigga Ground, the slave cemetery in the mountains of Goldsborough.

Living History – as recounted by Goldburn Job – The History Man

THE TRIANGULAR TRADE
Dirty Money

"According to tradition, ships sailed for Africa with holds full of idols and brass bracelets while the cabins were occupied by missionaries – an edifying example of material goods in competition with the immaterial one. The same ships carried slaves from Africa to the Caribbean and the U.S.A and sugar, rice and cotton from the regions to Europe, an immensely profitable triangular trade route.

Thousands of cargo ships participated in The Triangular Slave Trade; vessels from Sweden, Holland, France, Spain, Portugal, England and the U.S had names like 'Jesus', 'Gift of God', 'Amistad', 'Liberty', 'Justice' – a mockery to the captives, who had to live in the floating hell-hole dungeons, often for more than 10 weeks. Up to 30% would perish on the high seas"...

Eric Williams – Capitalism & Slavery

The Catholic Church received a Baptising fee for every captured and transported African. The Dutch Reform Church defended and justified slavery with the scriptures e.g. Thy Bondsmen and thy Bondmaids which thou shalt have, shall be of the heathen that are round about you....
Leviticus XXV, 44-45"

The European Transatlantic Slave Trade was a trade – through warfare, trickery, banditry and kidnapping"....Walter Rodney

MURDER MOST FOUL

It being the rule in the Colony of Suriname, that by paying a fine of 100 Florins (less than 50 pounds) per head, you are at liberty to kill as many negroes as you please...(Murder as Sport)

The training or 'seasoning' period lasted 3-4 years. Spirits were broken in order to transform the Africans into American/ Caribbean slaves. They were trained by other slaves or whites who had experience in 'breaking-in' even the most rebellious captives.

Mr. Ebbers was indeed particularly tyrannical, tormenting a boy of about 14 years of age...by alternately flogging him for 1 month, then keeping him laid down flat on his back with his feet in the stocks for another month, then making him wear a pot hook around his neck to prevent him from escaping or sleeping. This pot hook triangle was frequently put on negroes, which being formed with three long barbed spikes, to prevent them from entering the woods without getting entangled or sleeping in a sitting position.

Many devices were invented to prevent slaves from running away, including shackles and heavy collars. Slaves who eat more than their allotted ration could expect to be fitted with a device that covered their mouths.

I saw a black man hanged alive by the ribs, between which an incision was made with a knife and then a iron hook clinched with a chain. In this manner he kept living for 3 days, hanging with his head and feet downwards and catching with his tongue the drops of water (it being the rainy season) that were floating down his bloated breast while vultures were picking in the putrid wound.

Courtesy - Museum of Slavery, Curacao, Netherland Antilles.

AS RICH AS A
TOBAGO
PLANTER

In 1832, two years before the Emancipation Act freed 668,000 African slaves in the British West Indies, a list of Tobago Estates producing coconuts, cocoa, indigo, tobacco and sugar cane amounted to 75 in number. The largest amounts of slaves were employed on the following Estates:-

Les Coteaux - 436   Golden Grove - 357   Castara - 328   Lowlands - 301   Buccoo - 271   Richmond - 270   Courland - 264   Bacolet - 258   Goldsborough - 257   Auchenskeoch -   240   Shirvan - 235   Hope - 225   Charlotteville - 222   Riseland & Arnos Vale - 217 each   Betsey's Hope - 215   Runnemede - 211   Bon Accord - 210

Data kind courtesy La Magdalena by David Phillips

The slaves were subject to serve as 'Apprentices' to the said Masters for another 4 years until the Emancipation Act became Law on the 1st August 1838.

These slave masters were paid 20 million pounds sterling as compensation- - - - -the equivalent of approx. 12 billion pounds sterling or 24 billion U.S. $ or 144 billion $TT today.

Africans and their descendants were never compensated. The freed slaves were left to fend for themselves and it is to their eternal credit that these generational sons and daughters of the victims of humanity's most heinous crimes in the history of mankind, surpassing by no little margin the Jewish holocaust of 6 million innocent souls- - - -It is to their credit that they have risen up to freely and happily welcome all nations and all peoples to the island that their forbearers built.

William Wilberforce, the Yorkshire abolitionist through whose tenacity the Emancipation Act was eventually passed, did not live to see this day as he died in 1833.

"Those island societies would not exist as they do today were it not for Britain, and Britain would certainly not exist as it does today were it not for those islands".
Courtesy Andrea Levy – Winner of the Walter Scott prize for Historical Fiction 2011.

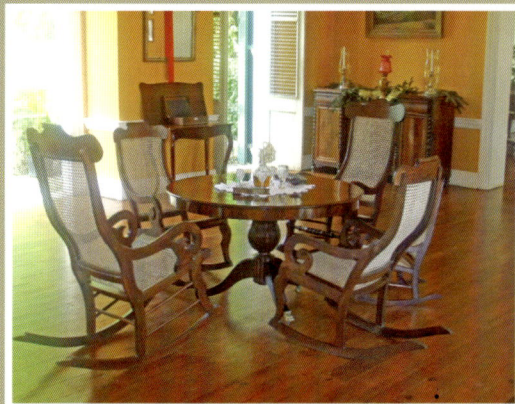

The **Slavery** Chronicles

GREAT BRITAIN ABOLISHES THE SLAVE TRADE 1807

An Independent Member of Parliament from Yorkshire, William Wilberforce introduced his first Abolition Bill in 1789, which created a movement that greatly influenced the U.S. Congress to ban the importation of slaves from Africa to the U.S. some two decades later. Strong opposition from the West Indian sugar lobby had delayed and frustrated the efforts of Wilberforce and his supporters, but in 1807 Royal assent was finally given to the Bill. *It took another 25 years for Parliament to finally abolish slavery in all British Territories.*

As the reliance on sugar production was so great in the various islands, another souce of almost free labour was required if the sugar industry was to continue to be sustained. East Indians from India were offered land in return for their labour under an Agreement of Indentureship which replaced the free slaves on the sugar plantations in some territories like Trinidad and Guyana.

Tobago
History

The Release from Slavery
Free at Last! – But don't get too excited about it, or else!

Proclamation – by His Excellency Major General Henry Darling, Lt. Governor of Tobago to the slave population – Government House, Tobago 1833.

"Knowing how much you all wish for the receipt of those orders, which you have for a long time expected, to release you from Slavery and make you free, I have great satisfaction in announcing to you that the Parliament of Gt. Britain has at last, after a great deal of trouble, completed the Laws & Regulations that have been found necessary on the great change, that is about to take place in your condition; and the King's orders which I have received to make known this to you, shall be immediately obeyed as soon as the proclamation can be printed and sent round the island.

To prevent you however from forming hasty and wrong opinions upon the subject, and then meeting with disappointment, I think it right to inform you that no change what ever will take place in your condition, until after next crop time, and that when your Slavery itself shall cease you will still be required to work for a certain time, for your former masters, but under Regulations different from those to which you have been hitherto accustomed.

I have directed all Managers, Overseers and Magistrates – in short all white people throughout the island, to explain such parts of the new law as are most interesting to you: if you are not satisfied with what they tell you, you may come to me for explanation, but take care that you do not come in greater numbers than two or three together. I will not receive or speak to any body of Slaves, either coming with complaints or to ask for information that may exceed that number.

I have now only to express my hope and desire that you will not allow the receipt of this intelligence, to excite you to any acts of Insubordination, Idleness or Riot.

It will be my duty, (which you may depend upon it I will not neglect) to support the Laws to the utmost and that any ill disposed Negroes who may absent themselves from their work, or advise others to do wrong, shall be selected as the fittest objects for severe example".

Ah well....Major Darling wasn't such a darling after all!!

Courtesy La Magdalena by David Phillips – Available from Island Investments 639 9901

Origins of some Place Names

Jan de Moor (a street near Carnbee Junct) was the Agent for the immensely wealthy Courteen Brothers, Dutch traders who operated from London. He was a merchant adventurer and later became a director of the Dutch West Indian Co., holding rights to bring settlers to Tobago.

Dutch Fort – This uphill street faces the **Scarborough Port** and was so named due to the fort that was erected by the Dutch settlers in 1662 to protect their settlement at **Rockly Bay**, which they called Roodlyp Bay.

The British captured the fort in 1666, but one year later, after the French drove out the Brits, the Dutch erected a new township, **Lower Scarborough**, which they called Lampsiusburg, after the Lampsius brothers, the wealthy merchant financiers of their expedition.

In 1821, the foundation stone of the Court House and Admin. Building was laid by Governor Robinson (**Robinson Street**); it overlooked the Market Sq. now known as **James Park** (after A.P.T. James, Tobago's charismatic rep. to Trinidad's legislature), whose bust is displayed in the square.

Chapter 7
RELIGION
& FOLKLORE

EBENEZER
METHODIST
CHURCH

CARIBBEAN CHURCHES

T&T's ethnic mix is mirrored in the varied numbers of religious organizations that thrive here. The older larger ones, Catholics and Anglicans, came to these Islands as colonists and built two grand Gothic Cathedrals in Trinidad's capital in the early 19th century. Include them in your photo shoots as well as Tobago's oldest Anglican Church – consecrated 1843 – St. Patrick at Mt. Pleasant, just a couple of minutes drive from Morshead supermarket. It was built with slave labour, the stones from England being delivered at Mt. Irvine Bay.

The East Indians were transported to Trinidad (not Tobago) as agricultural labourers when slavery was abolished. They brought with them their ancient religions of Hinduism and Islam, building their temples of worship (mandirs and mosques) while holding steadfast to their major religious festivals – Divali, Phagwa, Eid and Hosay. These festivals are held island-wide in Trinidad and specialist tour operators are your best and safest bets to experience their spiritual delights.

Locally, you can see   Tobago's traditionally styled
Mosque at Lowlands   near to the back gate of the
                                                          Hilton Hotel.

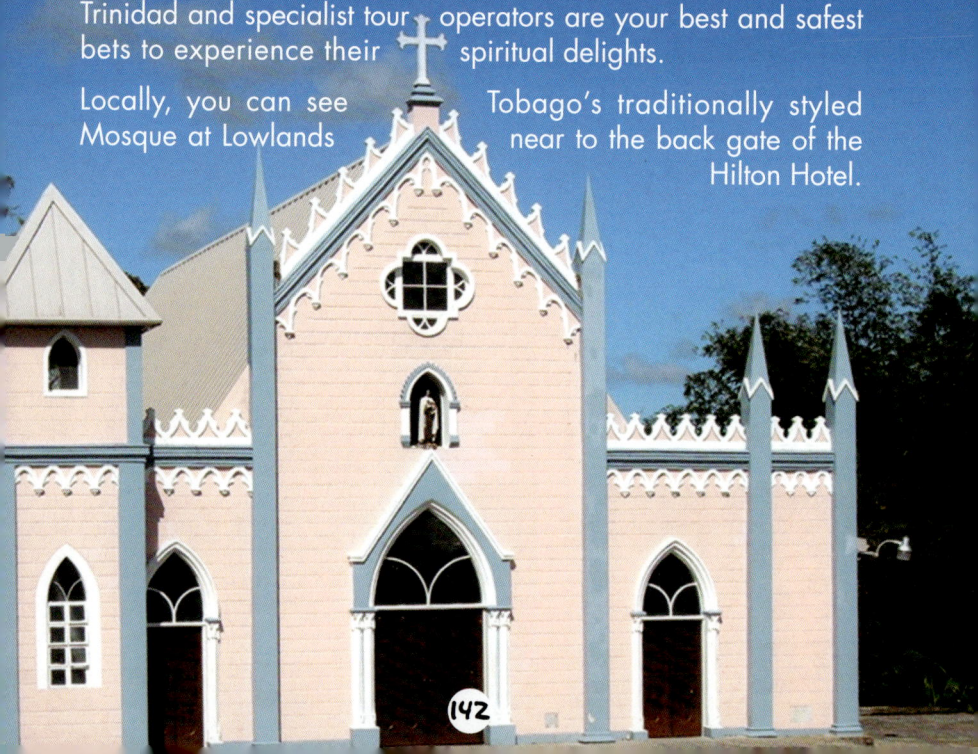

Tobago Folks –
Christian to the Bone

In Tobago, as on virtually all of the English speaking islands, one will find a multitude of Christian churches of various denominations built, maintained and attended by the majority of the islanders of African origin.

Unity of the Brethren

At the close of the 18th century a unique group of missionaries from Eastern Europe, followers of the reformist John Hus, who was martyred (burnt at the stake in 1415), founded the Moravian Church in Tobago and after enormous trials and tribulations began to contribute to the general improvement of the lives of the slaves by building schools (the first at Mt.Gomery) and teaching skills like music, sewing and building trades in many of the villages, some of which retain the names that originated from the Moravian faith – Moriah, Salem and Bethesda to name a few.

Beautifully restored examples of their original churches can be found at Black Rock, opposite the Anglican Church and also at Spring Garden on Orange Hill Road.

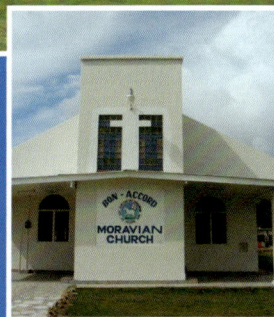

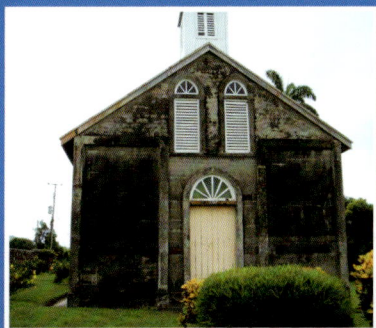

The Seventh Day Adventists, whose Sabbath falls on Saturday and the Methodists, are also providers of schools and educational pursuits in a religious landscape dotted with diverse Ministries, Assemblies, Evangelists and Pentecostalists.

cont'd over

Baptist Liberation

The Spiritual Baptists are the most African in their devotional manifestations and are easily identified by their occasional wayside services and colourful flowing robes, head-ties and flags fluttering proudly on the church compounds.

This Christian religious group, also known as Shouter Baptists, emerged among the African populace in T&T and was forced to go underground to practice their faith when a Prohibition Ordinance was passed in 1917 by the then Colonial Government prohibiting their mode of worship which was considered "too noisy, too African and therefore uncivilised and unacceptable."

The Ordinance virtually criminalized the sect until 1951 when the Order was repealed. The history and beliefs of this marginalized community were completely vindicated when in 1996, the Government declared March 30th an annual Public Holiday to be known henceforth as 'Spiritual Baptist/Shouter Liberation Day'.

Oft-times by the seaside, you may witness the continuing tradition of Baptism that originated at the birth of the Christian Movement on the banks of the Jordan River with the Baptism of its author and founder Jesus Christ by John the Baptist.

'The flowers in the bowl by the candlelight
looking pretty pretty, in the warm moonlight.
The songs that they singing
and the hands that they clapping
Lord, they sound so nice.
Take me home, River Jordan'..............

Copyright

Baptist Source – By kind courtesy of 'My Faith, Spiritual Baptist Christian' by Teacher H.A. Gibbs De Peza – University of the West Indies, School of Ed. Trinidad.

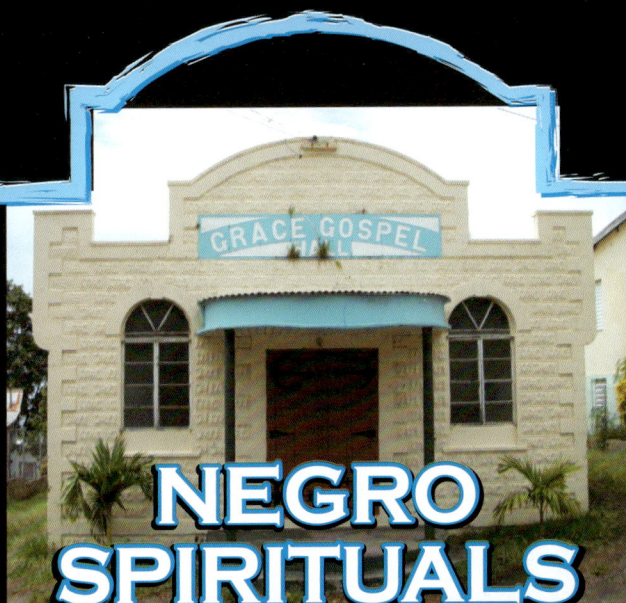

NEGRO SPIRITUALS

They made me work, oh yes, ah work so hard each day.
Lord, I'm die...ah...ing
Yes, I'm die...ah...ing
O Lord – I just wanna be FREE!
'The Slave' – Mighty Sparrow

Not too difficult to imagine that the human spirit would need a daily dose of hope and release from the horrors of slaving under the whip and the gun in the broiling sun-up to sun-down.

The work songs they created helped to ease the pain during daytime weekdays; and nighttime Sundays they would run off deep into the fields and woods to pray in song and chant for deliverance – Redemption Songs!!

On the North American continent, Man's inhumanity to Man created the music we know today as Negro Spirituals aka Gospel Music.

You can still hear it in abundance cascading into the streets from this island's Gospel Halls and Ministries each and every Sunday and some days in between.

CARIBBEAN HISTORY. . .
RASTAFARI

A Jamaican Creation – A Caribbean Phenomenon

Holiday on any Caribbean island and two images are sure to remain in the consciousness of the traveller – the vibrant colours of the Red, Gold & Green that decorate many roots shops, articles of clothing and crafts and also that other signature trademark - dreadlocks.

The Rastafarian movement's popularity owes much to Bob Marley its greatest ambassador. In Marley's own words – *"Rastaman vibrations gon' cover the earth, like water cover the sea"*.

For masses of poor, disillusioned and dispossessed, the messages conveyed in Rasta music's conscious lyrics act like a magnet to ordinary folks worldwide.

It all began in the 1920's and 30's when Jamaican Marcus Garvey encouraged Black Pride and repatriation to Africa for the long suffering slave descendants of the U.S.A. and the Caribbean. He even started a shipping company – Black Star Liner to achieve these ends. His interpretation of a biblical prophecy, with which he promoted his message of "Look to Africa, for there a king shall be crowned", found fertile soil in the spiritual imagination of his followers with the coronation in 1930 of the Ethiopian Emperor, Haile Selassie I, the 225th monarch in an unbroken line descending from the union of King Solomon and the Queen of Sheba. The followers viewed Ras (Prince) Tafari Selassie as God Incarnate on Earth and began to refer to His Imperial Majesty as Jah (Yahweh), The Conquering Lion of Judah.

Years later, Marley immortalized the speech Selassie made to the U.N, recalling Mussolini's invasion of Ethiopia, when he sang the Emperor's words as the lyrics for his song 'War' – *"Until the philosophy which holds one race superior and another inferior, is finally and permanently discredited and abandoned; until the colour of a man's skin is of no more significance than the colour of his eyes, me say War, Everywhere is War".*

In 1975, upon the passing of the beloved Emperor, Marley created and sang the Rasta Anthem *"Jah live(s)"* as a balm to the followers of the faith in the firm belief that Jah no dead- *"Children Yeah, Jah Jah live(s)".*

The wearing or growing of Dreadlocks is the most visible mark of Rastafarians.

The colours, red for the blood of martyrs, green for the lush vegetation and gold for the wealth and riches of Africa are worn with pride and often combined with black, in honour and memory of Marcus Garvey who started it all with his rallying calls – "Africa for Africans at home and abroad" and "Repatriation is a must".

So, next time you purchase an item bearing the colours of Rastafari, remember the true story and meaning behind its origins.

Rastafarians follow several basic doctrines – a mainly vegetarian (ital) salt-free diet which includes fish; shellfish and pork are forbidden, as is alcohol. The promotion of world peace and harmony is high on the agenda, while global repatriation remains on a distant horizon. For many years now, a thriving community of Rastas has been established in Shashamane, Ethiopia - lands courtesy of the late Ethiopian Emperor – Ras Tafari Selassie the First.

Now that's what I'd call a Happy Ending!

Marcus Mosiah Garvey

Jamaica's First National Hero was brought to the attention of later generations, when the reggae singer Burning Spear, who also came from the St. Ann's North Coast district, immortalised him in his beautiful classic composition – "No one remembers old Marcus Garvey, no one":....

It took the reggae world by storm in the 70's and still remains today the highlight of Spear's world wide performances.

Marcus Garvey had created a vibrant organization – Universal Negro Improvement Association to spread his message of Black Pride and self determination throughout the U.S.A and the Caribbean where blacks represented the largest and cheapest available labour force. The Establishment on both sides of the Atlantic mounted a 'dirty tricks' campaign to discredit and criminalise him for daring to threaten the status quo.

Liberty Hall, bought in 1923 by the Association's Kingston Division as its H.Q was restored and declared a National Monument by Jamaica's National Heritage Trust and the site deemed a Heritage Site. This legacy contains the Marcus Garvey multi-media museum and the research and reference library.

It is to Garvey's credit that thousands of Garveyites have heeded his call and repatriated themselves to their Mother Land.

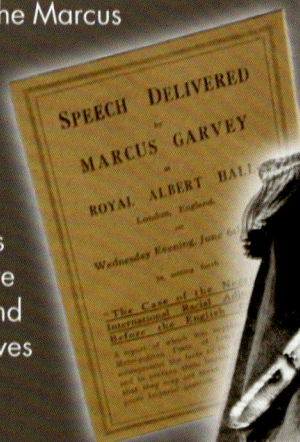

SHIRVAN PLAZA

Krackers The Restaurant
For Crazy Good Grilled Food

Reynaldo's Sports Bar

The Female Executive

Jo Jo's Cuisine

TAG Framing & Design

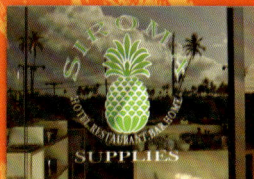

SIROMA SUPPLIES

C.P.A. Computers

Koral Boutique

Joy's Variety Store

Shirvan Road, Lowlands, Tobago. Tel. : 631-1133

Divali
DIVINE CREATIVITY
Hindu Festival of Light

Pronounced – (dee-waal-ee), it's the second biggest national open air festival held mainly in Trinidad, where Hindus comprise the second largest religious group after the Catholics. The world famous Trinidad carnival, with its Catholic background is the largest annual event, but the two events share a common passion for participation and attendance.

However, Divali is a spiritual, religious, alcohol free and vegetarian festival that celebrates the triumph of light over darkness, knowledge over ignorance and good over evil. Gifts, garlands and greeting cards are exchanged as would occur at Christmas time.

Millions of deyas (clay lamps) are lit in homes, streets, parks, offices and temples and decoratively displayed on split bamboo tubes with performances by singers, musicians, drummers, actors and models. Sweetmeats by the ton are enjoyed and distributed freely and people take to the streets or drive around to enjoy the sparklers, fireworks and the splendor of the illuminations.

Divali

Indian Bazaars and the crowning and showering with gifts of a Divali Queen as the best dressed fashion finalist are all part of the exciting celebrations.

Lord Rama, a most widely worshipped Hindu deity is responsible for the beginning of this tradition. It is related that upon his return from exile to his father's kingdom of Ayodhya, the people illuminated the town with rows of lights to welcome him back and girls tossed fragrant flowers from windows and roof tops. Lord Rama's story is to be found in the epic poem 'Ramayana' and the drama of 'Rama Leela' unfolds over 9 nights on royal stages in central Trinidad at the Divali Nagar.

Ordinary villagers play a multitude of celestial roles in glitzy costumes and always you will hear the thunderous beating of the mighty Tassa drums.

The story of Lord Rama has enthralled millions of people since it was composed some 6,000 years ago by the poet Valmiki.

The Female deity Mother Lakshmi is also given special worship at this time as befitting the Goddess of Light, Wealth and Wisdom and lamps are lit to invoke her presence and light her path to the homes of the devoted.

Spiritual tourism at its finest – Enjoy T&T

Tobago Tour Guides can arrange with their Trinidad counterparts for couples and groups to be escorted and attend the celebrations.

Christmas Time

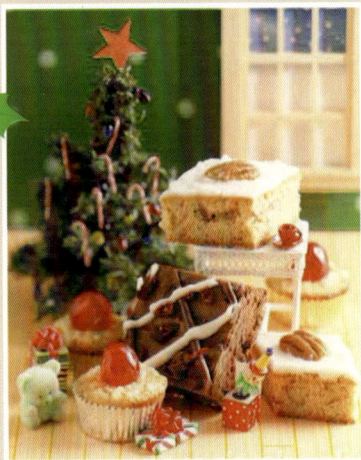

Although it is a Christian festival, all religions and peoples of the Island celebrate and enjoy Christmas.

But, before Christmas can be enjoyed to the full, for the weeks leading up to the festivities, nobody can escape the frenzy of cleaning house, painting, sewing new curtains etc. that is an essential part of the pre-Christmas activities. There are lots of home-made traditional treats and drinks, such as Pastels, Fruit Cake, Punche de Crème, Ham with mustard pickle, Ginger Beer and Sorrel, a refreshing drink made from the red flower of the Sorrel plant, to mention a few. Church services, visiting neighbours and family are usual activities. Boxing Day is usually spent in leisurely pursuits and beach outings while New Year's Eve is referred to as Old Year's Night and is celebrated in the usual way with fireworks etc. The kids make bamboo canons so don't be alarmed if you hear loud explosions coming from the Villages. Its called 'bussing bamboo'.

Look out for the pre-Christmas Caravan, which rolls into the Villages at the weekends delivering Calypso-flavoured Carols and Spanish Parangs, courtesy of the Culture Department. Go on the 'What's on..' Website Calendar for details. **Not to be missed!!**

TOBAGO HARVEST FESTIVALS

Harvest Festivals are traditional celebratory occasions in Tobago's Island life centered around the four mainstream Christian Churches; Anglican (C of E), Roman Catholic, Methodist and Moravian. Harvest Time served as a way of raising funds for the Church, parishioners proudly bringing their best produce in place of monetary tithes.

Houses would be spruced up and decorated, with much baking and cooking and thanking the Lord for His bountiful blessings. Folks took the opportunity to visit family and friends and stay the weekend, affirming the unity of Christians as brothers and sisters. The Anglican Church tradition, for example, features a Eucharistic service in the morning when the best produce is brought to the Church followed by a Cantata in the early afternoon when the choirs and other talented members make their musical contributions. The Moravian Church has a long history of missionary work on the Island, building schools and teaching music, sewing skills and building trades to various communities. The village of Mt. Gomery is named after the first Moravian Missionary and the villages of Bethesda, Salem (De Vignes Rd) and Moriah are names originating from the Moravian faith, which has sought to contribute to the general improvement of the lives of Tobagonians.

So, if you would like to spend a pleasant Sunday in the company of your warm Tobago hosts, get yourself along to a Harvest and join in the spirit of love and the brotherhood/sisterhood of Mankind.

Log on to www.visittobago.gov.tt to see a list of Harvest Festival dates.

153

CRUSOE'S ISLE
Fiction to Fact?

Almost 300 years ago in April 1719, English author David Defoe created the legend of Crusoe by the publication of a fictitious tale that gripped the imagination of a world fixated with the age of geographical discovery. He named his work "The Life & Strange Surprising Adventures of Robinson Crusoe of York – Mariner", which became an instant best seller, causing Defoe to attempt further sequels.

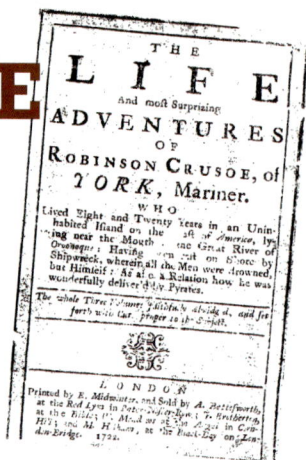

The first of these contained Crusoe's adventures after his eventual discovery and rescue by a crew of mutineers and also accounted the death of Man Friday, the noble tribal Indian killed by three arrows while acting as the interpreter on an expedition to 'The Brazils'. Upon his return to England Crusoe had also married, but shortly after was sadly widowed.

Though not mentioned by name, the writer leaves the readers in no doubt as to the identification of Tobago as the island home of the sole shipwrecked survivor, a mariner marooned for 28 years on an uninhabited tropical island.

Over the years, Tobago came to be known as Crusoe's Isle. You can find references to this classic story in the form of various commercial place names on the island – there is even a local Calypso singer who goes by the name -Tobago Crusoe!

Explore more! Enjoy more!

T&T FOLKLORE

Legends, Myths & Superstitions - Part I

It was once a common rural pastime for families and neighbours to gather round the outdoor fire at night, roasting and eating nuts and corn while recounting tales and superstitions much to the fearful delight of the children. Here is one such Tobago legend........................

GANG GANG SARAH

Legend has it that one stormy night Sarah flew from Africa and landed in the Tobago village of Les Coteaux, from where she journeyed to Golden Lane in search of her family who had been transported there as slaves. There she resided and was the loving wife of Long Tom, who legend says she had known as a child in her native Africa. She lived to a ripe old age and when Tom died she thought that she would return to Africa. However, her diet would naturally contain salt as most diets do, and the story goes that she climbed the Silk Cotton tree but was unable to fly back as she had eaten salt. It's believed that she is buried under this tree, and to this day the names of Tom and Sarah can been seen inscribed upon two headstones in Golden Lane.

This story has become part of Tobago's folk lore, and you can find the ancient tree on the way to Footprints Eco Resort. There are many interesting versions told of the legend of Gang Gang Sarah.

Picture – Kind Courtesy Paria Publishing Co. Ltd.

Legends, Myths & Superstitions - Part II

In the folklore of these Islands there are a few characters, some of whom have distant parallels with European counterparts. The female vampire, Soucouyant, is one such and like some others they are known by their French names – French patois being a dominant language spoken in lots of the Caribbean islands in earlier times.........Still is, in their former colonies, Haiti, Martinique, St. Lucia, Guadeloupe, French St. Martin and parts of the Grenadines.

THE SOUCOUYANT took the form of a ball of fire floating on the wind and in the middle of the flames would be seen the face of an old witch looking for people in order to suck their blood. The victims would awaken with black and blue discolourations where they had been sucked and usually died after a prolonged bout of weakness and frailty. The Soucouyant was portrayed as an old crone who lived alone and in order to achieve the transformation, had to leave her skin behind in a mortar. She would return home just before daylight and if the villagers had plucked up enough courage to enter her home and find the mortar and were to sprinkle coarse salt and pepper on the skin, she would not be able to attain the retransformation and would therefore die a horrible death.

Legends, Myths & Superstitions - Part II cont'd

THE SOUCOUYANT *(cont'd)* - It was also believed that if one were to empty a bag of rice at the village crossroads, the Soucouyant was obliged to stop on her way home and pick up each grain, where upon on the onset of daybreak the villagers would discover her and her true identity.

LA DIABLESSE (DEVIL WOMAN) possesses a cloven hoof in place of a normal foot, the other foot being fashionably shod. She is usually very attractive and well perfumed, dresses in the mode of the embroidered lace costumery of the French islands with an elaborate turban, golden necklaces and ear-rings. She preys on single men making their way home at night, usually after a night out having a good time. She trails an old iron chain, a heritage of her slavery days and it is believed that she represents the spirit of the woman wronged, wreaking vengeance on would-be male predators.

She seduces the young men, leading them on, as aflame with desire, they follow her into the high woods never to return, or if they do, it is as raving lunatics. In the Voodoo cult, she is worshiped as the re-creation or Erzulie, the tragic West African goddess. The lore may have been brought to these islands by French slaves from St. Lucia and Haiti in the late 1700's.
Don't stay out late, young fella!

The river hole

By Leslie Palmer

Father Michael woke up early, and as he knew the river, he walked down the hill and decided to bathe at first light and meditate in the beauty and stillness of the morning dew.

As he reached down the gully bank and glad to be there with the solitude, who could he see, with she back to him, but a black woman standing up naked, waist deep in the middle of the shallows. She black, she shine, she hair long and she back smooth and broad. She scrubbing she-self and not concerned with nothing else, so Father Michael have to cough to let she know he see she.

So she turn and hold she breasts and sit down in the water to hide she-self and the good Father crossed the river on the stones laid down for that purpose and turn his face to the sun thru' the trees to compose he-self and meditate on the sins of mankind – in this case womankind. She breasts full and they remain in Father mind – a beauty of the purest kind.

He get confused and it seemed like by the time he turn around, she standing next to him, dressed and black and flash she teeth and she eye and Father face flushed red right down to his crucifix.

Father get more confused and he forget that the pool now empty and he coulda take his swim right there so he start walking down the river bank with the woman behind. She have a real sweet laugh and she bust it from time to time and it make Father relax as it blend in wid the sounds of the river and the birds trilling in the morning air.

"Is not far" – she say and give a little laugh but when Father ask her does she go to Church and if she lives in the village, he never get an answer, so he thinks it's his thick Irish brogue dat she don't understand.

In a little while they reach another water hole and it pleased Father to find it vacant and inviting in its beauty. When he turn round to thank her for taking him, Father find himself alone. At the same time he hears a horse gallop in the bush and as he turn to his left to see what coulda make this noise, his foot slipped on the moss on the rock and he fall in the water hole. He hit the back of his head as he somersaulted, and the last thing he heard in the short space of his life was the woman laughing, clear as the Irish crystal mingling with the Church bells that were calling the faithful to mass.

From that day, when they found Father Michael drowned in the pool, the people in the Village named the river hole St. Michael, and from that time is only the priest from the Abbey that used to bathe there. The Village old people say Father Michael did follow a La Diablesse and that's why he dead, but the priests from the Abbey above didn't believe in any such foolishness.

'The River Hole" taken from the booklet of short stories "Holiday Shorts – Just Right for the Beach" available from Gift Shops island wide.

T&T FOLKLORE

Legends, Myths & Superstitions - Part III

DUENNES (PRONOUNCED DWENS) are the mischievous spirits of un-baptised children who lure living children away into the forest where they are then abandoned. They take the form of sexless children without faces except for a little mouth. Their feet are turned backwards and they wear outsized straw hats upon their large heads. They are wont to steal the names and mannerisms of their intended victims, particularly at dusk. Mothers use this myth to frighten their kids into staying indoors once darkness falls.

PAPA BOIS (FATHER OF THE WOODS) is the guardian of the forests and protector of its animals. He appears in various forms, mostly with a leafy beard and cloven feet, sometimes as a deer, but mostly as a muscular, hairy old man in raggedy clothes, blowing a cow horn to warn the animals of the hunters' approach. It is as a deer that he tricks the hunters to follow him into the deep forest where he reveals himself in his true form in order to berate them, leaving them lost before vanishing.

MAMAN DE L'EAU (WATER MOTHER) could very well be the first 'Eco-activist', as she's known to take her revenge on men who pollute rivers, burn and fell trees or kill forest animals. Her lower half takes the form of a giant Anaconda snake, but she can also be transformed into a beautiful belle, quietly singing as she sits on the river bank. She is thought to be the lover of the forest's keeper, the ultimate Eco Warrior Papa Bois.

Should you be so unlucky to encounter her - *remove your shoes, turn them up-side-down and walk barefoot backwards until you reach home!!*

EATING OUT

Chapter 8
LOCAL FOODS
& EATING OUT

TODAYS SPECIAL

Cowheel Soup
Pig Tail Soup
Vegetable Soup
Fish Broth
Grill Salads
Sandwiches

OPEN
TODAY'S SPECIAL
LUNCHES
**HOT
ROTI**
DAILY
• SHRIMPS • FISH
• CHICKEN • BEEF
• DUCK • GOAT • CONCH

IN THE
MARKETPLACE
BLUE FOOD & OTHER DELIGHTS

Welcome to the world of starchy roots and tubers that are staple diet here on these Caribbean islands. You will certainly see mounds of them in the markets, but a little less likely to find them on your hotel dinner menu except, perhaps for the sweet potato and fried plantain. However, if and when you 'eat local', so to speak, you will surely be intrigued by the taste of these underground delights that have been cooked up here for centuries. These examples are collectively known as 'ground provisions'. It might be that one has to acquire the taste in order to appreciate the full flavours of these 'provisions'.

Cassava – was brought to the islands by the indigenous Indians of South America. It has a thick, shiny bark, boils easily and is a good accompaniment to a salt fish dish. Tapioca pudding is made from this root as well as the ancient practice of grating cassava to produce cassava bread – another treat learnt from the Indians of the vast Amazon basin.

Dasheen – aka Taro turns blue when boiled and gave rise to the term 'blue food', which generally refers to the veggies you are reading about in this article. There are a couple of close

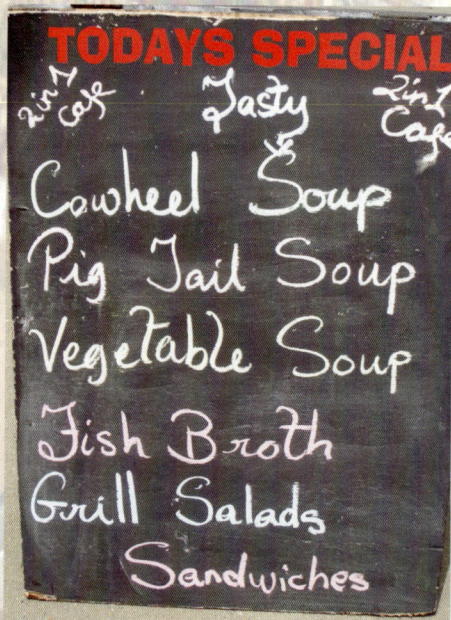

TODAYS SPECIAL

2in1 Cafe   Tasty   2in1 Cafe

Cowheel Soup
Pig Tail Soup
Vegetable Soup
Fish Broth
Grill Salads
Sandwiches

relatives i.e. Tannia and Eddoes, but the Dasheen's leaves are the ones used for that most mouthwatering appetizer – Callaloo Soup.

Yams – can grow underground to rather large proportions and unusual shapes and originated in Africa, where they can be prized possessions. Unlike the sweet potato and cassava, which have traditional shrub-like branches and leaves, yams grow from vine-like plants and can take a year to fully mature. They are enjoyed boiled, mashed and fried like potatoes.

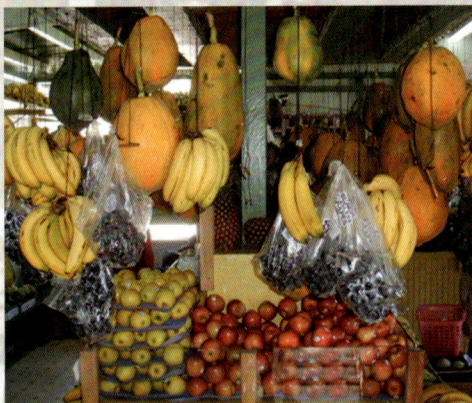

Plantains – unlike those above, plantains grow above ground and look like giant bananas; however, they need to be cooked before eating. The green and half ripe ones should be boiled and the deep yellow ripe specimens can be fried or baked in their skins. It is usual to slice the ribbed edges of the thick skin before boiling in its jacket.

Green Bananas – locally known as 'green figs'. Europeans would know figs as a multi-seeded Mediterranean fruit, which can be eaten fresh or dried; but for some unknown reason, Caribbean peoples tend to refer to the various varieties of bananas, which vary from 2 to 9 inches in length as figs!

At the market place or green grocer you can buy a 'hand of green figs' ready for boiling as you would potatoes, in their jackets or peeled. They're eaten with other 'provisions' as a side dish, but can also take the place of rice in a meal. Boiled, (they are never, ever to be eaten raw as you would a ripe banana) they can be mashed and used in a pie, or cut-up and used just like potatoes in a green-fig salad, or stewed in a coconut curry sauce. *Gourmet Heaven at the Blue Food Fest annually in October.*

Some Tobago Fruits
that we eat, suck and drink

ARISE, SIR BREADFRUIT
SOUPY SATURDAYS

The size of a junior football, breadfruit is high in starch and calories and can be cooked in various ways. This versatility, as well as the ability to grow in tropical areas and its abundant production capabilities made it a valuable resource for slave owners with many mouths to feed. Plants were transported from their native Polynesia to St. Vincent by the legendary Capt. Bligh and distributed to other islands.

Joseph Robley, Tobago's most prominent planter at Golden Grove was awarded the Society of Arts medal for his success in propagating breadfruit trees. The slaves preferred plantains and it took some time for them to accept breadfruit as part of their diet.

Breadfruit eventually became staple diet on plantations throughout these sun-kissed islands, where they are still enjoyed today.

The white sap, secreted from its trunk when cut, makes an ultra strong waterproof gum and is a favourite with rural boys in Trinidad to snag song-birds, while its leaves and flowers are used for medicinal herbal teas.

No self respecting pea-soup is complete without salted beef/pork and the ubiquitous breadfruit. Its light yellow meaty pulp is simmered down with coconut milk to produce a perennial favourite known locally as 'Oil-down'.

Boiled, baked, fried or roasted the humble breadfruit remains a firm favourite on these culinary appreciative shores.

Try local food outlets when the local tradition of Soup on Saturday is usually on their lunchtime menus. *Arise, Sir Breadfruit!*

DE BOSS AH... SOUP

Soup Everyday!

The history of soup is probably as old as the history of cooking. The act of combining various ingredients in a large pot to create a nutritious, filling, easily digested and simple to make food. This type of preparation made it the perfect choice for both sedentary and traveling cultures, rich and poor, healthy people and invalids. Soup has evolved according to local ingredients and tastes. Rich, hearty and delicious soups are a major part of Creole cooking – and each island has its own unique dishes. Tasting soup here on Tobago is like tasting a piece of the island's heritage, where the flavours can be traced back hundreds of years.

In Trinidad and Tobago, soup was the traditional Saturday lunch, where everything in the ice box was brought together to make a nutrient rich meal for families. It meant the ice box was empty, ready to restock at the market on a Sunday. It is still a firm favourite today both with locals and visitors. Tobago has developed its own special soups. Chief among these are callaloo, corn, pigtail, cow heel and fish broth.

For the best soup on Tobago made with only the freshest and finest TnT ingredients and cooked how yuh want, visit De Boss Ah Soup at Stumpy's Compound in Canaan, Tobago or if in Trinidad at 48 Tragarete Road, Port of Spain - there are many imitators out there but remember if its not de Boss is not de Bess.

Soup Every Day...
the way the locals love 'em...

166

MANGOES...MANGOES... MANGOES

Ah want a penny to buy Mango Rose, Mango Teen

I've been told that you'll find Mango Mossy and John Buck Mangoes in Moriah and Suppie Mango, some say, grows in Bon Accord, while Button Mangoes, so called as they are small enough to get 2 or 3 in your mouth together, and are found only in Charlotteville.

Mangoes taste delightful what ever their names and T&T's no slouch when naming the numerous varieties of this juicy fruit found on these shores. The lines of the old folk song by Trinidad's Olive Walke tell you how seriously these folks take their Mangoes....................

Ah want a penny to buy
Mango Vert, Mango Teen
Mango Zabico, Calabash
Savez-vous all for me (save all for me).

Earlier, the French patois language was spoken extensively in many of the islands including Trinidad, so French words were often used to name the mangoes e.g. Mango Doux-Douce (sweet-sweet), Mango Vert (green).

It's been only 150 years since the East Indians were brought to Trinidad to work the sugar plantations as indentured labourers, and with them came all the different ways they pickled, preserved, curried and massala'd the green and almost ripe stages of the fruit. The Chinese immigrants to the island added

cont'd over

their own touch and the practice of adding colourings gave rise to a thriving confectionary business in the production of the bags of 'red mango' preserves sold in all tuck-shops and grocery stores on both islands, as well as in West Indian communities abroad.

I dare say these preserves have also made their way to Grenada and St. Vincent and other neighbouring islands as all these sun-kissed islands take their love of Mangoes to their hearts.

Here are some of the fanciful names we call 'em by................ Mango Starch, Little Pa, Ice Cream, Big Meat a.k.a Bellyfull, Rosy Cheek or Mango Rose, Cutlass, Custard, Long, Mango Spice, Mangoes Peter, Clementine and Graham Mango – not forgetting the Queen of all Mangoes – Julie Mango.

So next time you are out walking in the hotel grounds or the surrounding neighbourhood and discern Mangoes on the trees, ask a local which variety of these fanciful names you are seeing. Of course, there are Calypsos about Mangoes including classics by the late Lord Kitchener, 'I wish I was a Mango Tree, planted in Laventille' and The Mighty Sparrow's, 'If you suck it right, the hair won't stick in your teeth".

Hit the Scarborough market and you just might hear a vendor singing out.............
Mangoes!..........Mangoes!.........Mangoes!

TREE OF LIFE
THE COCONUT
PALM

They're a natural backdrop to Tobago's lush shore lines and are to be seen in abundance on many former estates where they were harvested and sold in Trinidad for the production of coconut oil and other by-products including soap and margarine.

Like cocoa and sugar cane their production and export potential eventually became uneconomical, but even so, coconuts remain the most commonly used floral resource as every part of the tree has some human usage.

Buoyant when dry, growing easily in sandy soil and found throughout the tropical world, they are spread great distances over the seas by maritime currents; exposure to wintry conditions is usually fatal.

"Get your coconut water,
It's good for your daughter,
Coco got a lotta iron,
Make you strong like a lion."

The refreshing coconut water from the green nut is a popular long, cold drink and a favourite mixer for rum. You can usually purchase the 'water nuts' at the Scarborough Market or in plastic bottles to take home from vendors.

The dry nut produces the most widely used cooking ingredient – coconut milk which is produced by squeezing the concoction produced by mixing warm water with the grated, fleshy meat of the dried seed. This milk is the liquid cooks and chefs use extensively to flavour meat and fish to give that wonderful coconut taste to certain dishes. When refrigerated, the cream rises to the top and is a richer more concentrated product that

169

cont'd over

can be sold in blocks like butter, hence **coconut cream**, sold world-wide in ethnic shops. In Tobago it's usually marketed in powder form as coconut cream powder.

The grated coconut meat is also used to make coconut candy and a variety of baked items like coconut bake, breads, cakes and tarts; coconut ice-cream is everyone's favourite.

Sturdy cricket bats for soft-ball games can be fashioned from the green or dried branches which are also used for thatching and fencing. The long plentiful leaves are used to weave baskets and sun hats. The ribs or spines of the long leaves, when bound together, make perfectly functional brooms; being light and flexible kids find them ideal for kite making.

The strong fibre from the dried husks i.e. the outside covering of the seed, is used to produce ropes, mats, brushes, stuffing and potting compost and is also an excellent source of fuel for cooking. The super hard shell is used for making buttons, bird feeders and coconut jewellery for the tourism trade and the trunks are cut into logs for use as posts in wooden home construction.

Finally, palm wine is made from the fermented sap of the flower clusters while from the roots of this amazing tree is derived a medicinal potion used in the treatment of dysentery.

Tree of Life, indeed!

GO BANANAS

You're sure to see them growing everywhere on the island, their huge purple bulbous flowers dangling and the fruit in large uniform green bunches; the plants produce one bunch of fruit from one flowering stem, then dies sending out new shoots called suckers.

They were brought to Europe by Portuguese sailors in the 15th century and then to the West Indies by the Spanish, but it's believed that Alexander the Great came upon them in India.

Bananas are perhaps the world's favourite fruit and can be served in any number of imaginative ways – from smoothies and punches to exotic cocktails or baked in breads or sliced and sprinkled over with brown sugar and served with a dollop of ice cream.

It's best to buy them with a slight green tinge and keep them away from direct sunlight to keep them from ripening too quickly. They are rich in Vitamin C, Potassium and Magnesium but low in fat.

You might like to try the other rarer varieties you'll find on sale at the market; they're smaller than the standard bananas and although they're not as common, they're just as sweet but with their own individual tastes – ask for 'silk figs' or 'c-key-a figs' (a forefinger in length) – fully ripe, these mutants will delight your taste buds.

Here's a local tip – Rub the inside of a banana skin on your mosquito bites to stop the itch.
Go Bananas…

"*Make mine a Pina Colada*"

Whether indulging yourself at breakfast, dessert, or poolside with the ubiquitous Pina Colada, the pineapple is very much part of the Caribbean vacation experience.

Just a few varieties of pineapple are actually sold in the global market place as whole fruits, while enormous numbers of slices and chunks are consumed from cans world-wide. They're harvested on almost every island, a consequence of the migratory habits of the indigenous Carib Indians who bartered them on their travels. The armour-like shell and ground level growing position make the pineapple a more suitable candidate for hurricane survival than papayas or bananas.

The Royal Botanical Gardens at Kew, on the outskirts of London, played a major role in cross-breeding plants to improve their sweetness and then returned the new hybrids to various locations throughout the Caribbean. The dominant variety in the Caribbean is the Red Spanish, which also goes by other names i.e. Antiguan Black, Guyana Joe, Dominica Green...............

You will find that the sweetness of this most fragrant and juicy fruit is enhanced when stored in the fridge and served cold.

How to make a delicious Pina Colada:-

1 1/2 ozs. Light or Dark Rum
2 ozs. Tinned Coconut Cream
2 ozs. Pineapple Juice
1 Cup Crushed Ice

Pour all ingredients into a blender and blend until smooth.
Serve with a slice of pineapple and a maraschino cherry.

Pina Colada anyone?

THE CULINARY & BLUE FOOD FESTIVALS

Both festivals encourage healthy competition between the chefs, not only in the preparation and presentation of their offerings, but also in the innovatory nature of their culinary delights.

The rural Blue Food Festival held in October in Bloody Bay is the hands-down winner in the latter division, while Pigeon Point's idyllic setting compliments the startling array of local concoctions and international dishes.

Ultimately, festival goers are the real beneficiaries.

Food glorious food!!

SOUSE

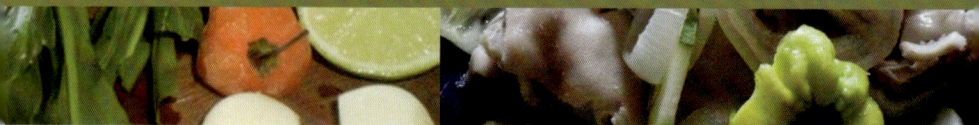

On any Friday, outside any large supermarket in Tobago, you will find ladies selling food ladelled out of large white plastic buckets into plastic cups. The main item on the Menu is SOUSE, a delicacy dating back to the times of slavery.

At the end of the harvesting of the sugar crop, the 'massa' and his family feasted and the bits that he did not relish would be sent down to the slave quarters and these bits included the feet or trotters, the tail and the head. The dishes that resulted in cooking these parts have become known as Heritage food and are seen as food for special occasions.

So the Souse being sold on Friday nights has a real history and a real flavour as well. Heritage foods are extremely tasty, showing just what can be done to 'unwanted' animal parts to make them into delicious dishes. The term 'souse' obviously comes from the European method of cooking fish in vinegar, so that it's not only very tasty but also preserved by the vinegar thus improving its keeping qualities. The slave cooks, having no vinegar used lime juice instead. Nowadays other meats are used as well as trotters although the latter remains a firm favourite - chicken feet, conch, pig's head and more recently, cow's skin. The reason given for the use of cow's skin for Souse is that here in Tobago there is no leather industry and the next best thing to do is to eat it!

The Recipe

Main ingredient…
Conchs or pig foot or chicken feet or pig's head or cow's skin

Souse ingredients
Limes
Scotch Bonnet Pepper (1)
Flavour Pepper
Cucumbers
Chives (Spring onions)
Salt

Any meats being used are chopped into bite sized pieces, washed in lime juice and left to stand for at least 5 minutes in the lime juice.

They are then boiled in salty water until tender…Hours if you are dealing with cow skin and as for conch; it is best pounded before cooking to tenderize it!

Meanwhile, wash, peel and slice the cucumbers, clean and chop the chives and de-seed and chop the flavour pepper. Mix these and add lime juice, hot pepper (whole if you want flavour and chopped if you want tears!) and salt. The latter should be added sparingly at first as the cucumbers tend to absorb it. Keep adding until the desired taste has been reached. To the cool meat add the lime juice/cucumber/chive mix. Keep in fridge or cool place until needed.

Just before serving add a little water if you want a liquidy souse; if you want to keep it fairly dry and relish the sucking of the meats to get the flavour, leave out the water.

Whatever you do check the saltiness and remove the hot pepper before it bursts.

Courtesy of Harriet's Cookery Book, a very popular local recipe book available from Khan's Booksellers @ Gulf City Mall, Tobago.

THE SEAHORSE INN
Restaurant & Bar

Regarded as a haven for romantics, foodies, and occasional visiting celebrities the restaurant is considered by most to be the jewel in the crown of Tobago Dining, featuring regularly in many international media productions and publications. Open seven nights a week, with entertainment on several evenings, reservations are essential throughout the year. Take our advice, book to go early during your stay as you will definitely want to return. **Tel: 639-0686 or seahorse@trinidad.net.**

Salsa Kitchen
Tapas Restaurant

Come and try our garlic bread with our variety of Tapas like, Sizzling Pork in a sweet and spicy "secret" Mint sauce or Dos Quesos- made up of local feta and mozzarella topped with an onion, caper and olive confit or a variety of salads like Caprese with fresh Tomatoes and Basil with authentic Buffalo Mozzarella and...... Iain's Rum Punch.

See Salsa Kitchen reviews in www.nytimes.com
- www.trinichow.com
- www.tripadvisor.co.uk

Marcia's Diner
Authentic Tobago Cuisine

Since its inception in 1983, Marcia has stayed true to her calling, expressing her natural God given talents by creating exceptionally well balanced, aesthetically-pleasing and enticing local cuisine. Some of her authentic dishes are Sunday Style Stewed Chicken, Lobster Tobago Style, Cedros Jumbo Shrimp and Tobago's Crab & Dumplings.

Reservations Tel: 639-0359

Shore Things Café & Craft

While the food, drinks and craft are reason enough to return to Shore Things again and again, the most frequently written comment in the guest book is about the wonderful service. The staff is friendly, helpful, always with a ready smile to welcome you to Shore Things Café & Craft.

Go on...indulge naturally.

BAKE & FISH and CRAB & DUMPLINGS
Home-made in T&T

Local chunky version of a fish sandwich; the bread used in this case being home-made coconut flavoured dough, roasted to perfection on a flat griddle over an open flame or baked in an enclosed oven, the end product being 1" to 1 1/2" thick and usually about 10" to 12" in diameter. Buttered hot, in pizza style triangles or served with a layer of cheese, they are staple breakfast fare for numerous households in T&T, as bakes are far more economical than purchasing supermarket bread.

Flying fish fillets and King fish cutlets are the usual fillings, but by far the most popular bake & fish combination is 'Bake & Shark', the shark being the unfortunate Reef shark; the younger the better as they are a virtually boneless fish anyway.

Try some roast bake with the popular Buljol filling (salt cod fish, served cold with tomatoes, onion, cucumber, olive oil and pepper sauce mixture) or deep-fried fritters of shredded cod fish mixed with herb-flavoured batter; notalgically referred to as Accra - the capital of Ghana on the Gold Coast from whence the African slaves were brought to T&T.

You won't have to look far to find some on these islands. Chase with an ice-cold drink of Mauby, the local tree bark coolant or a delicious fruit punch.

Crab & Dumplings is Tobago's National dish and consists of coconut flavoured curried crab served with traditional stiff flour and water dumplings. This delightful dish is a must-have item for visitors and the Store Bay beach food outlets all serve their own version. But, like the Roti, be prepared for a hands-on experience to get the best from the crab. ***Try some!***

RUM GLORIOUS RUM...
When ah call, yuh bound to come...

(Old drinking ditty)

It certainly goes hand in hand with the Caribbean vacation experience, as Caribbean rums are renowned the world over. So, when you find yourself in T&T consider yourself lucky to be able to sample a range of delightful rums made by, perhaps the leading distiller of the finest aged rums in the world. But don't take my biased word, just know that the Angostura 1919 brand won the 2005 Rum of the Year Award and that the 1824 brand was awarded the Gold Medal at the International Fair that judges these competitions.

What follows is the tale of the Island's foremost provider of this Nation's favourite tipple and also the background to a unique T&T product...Angostura Bitters®.

The story begins with Johann Siegert a Medical Doctor who left his German homeland in 1820 to join up with Simon Bolivar's army in Venezuela fighting against the Spanish throne. He was appointed Surgeon General of the Military Hospital in the town of Angostura, now known as Ciudad Bolivar. There he became a skilled Apothecary using medicinal roots and plants to cure the sick soldiers. One of his remedies was a concoction known as 'aromatic bitters'. He used his aromatic bitters to improve appetite and the digestive wellbeing of the soldiers. When added to food or drink, bitters has the ability to marry flavours bringing out the

cont'd over

best in them and just a few drops can enhance the flavour of any dish or drink.

He died in 1870 and his family emigrated to Trinidad where his eldest son begins to introduce the said product at foreign exhibitions. The family had some experience of rum making as they had produced a signature blend - Siegert's Bouquet Rum infused with bitters.

By 1900, the company had ventured into bottling rum from other distillers, but it wasn't until 1945 that they bought their own distillery and began producing fine rums on a major scale. A mere 15 years later, the company had extended distribution of its products to over 140 countries and had become well known Internationally for its high quality rums in addition to the now world famour Angostura Bitters®.

In 1985, Angostura Limited became the first company to be awarded T&T's highest National Award, the Humming Bird Medal for its contribution to Industry.

Angostura Bitters® has also been granted a Royal Warrant of Appointment which demonstrates excellence and quality and also indicates a universal seal of approval.

Today, there are Visitors' Tours at their complex, just outside Port of Spain, where one can view artifacts in their museum, gain an insight into the fascinating would of rum making and purchase merchandising products and of course bottles of their finest rums...and bitters.

Chapter 9
PIRATES IN THE CARIBBEAN

Pirates in the Caribbean
Life as a Pirate –
Rules to Live by (or die for)......

It is believed that pirate ships were generally run along democratic lines especially when important decisions were to be made. This majority rule policy deterred mutiny, but when at battle or on the rampage, the Captain held absolute power and to disobey his commands was to invite retribution.

Rule 1 – Everyone must obey the commands of the Captain.

Rule 2 – Everyone shall have a share of any treasure, but for every piece of gold a member of the crew is given, the Captain shall be given one and a half.

Rule 3 – If anyone steals or gambles they will be marooned with only a bottle of water and a pistol.

Rule 4 – Anyone who encourages a new pirate to join the crew without everyone else's agreement will suffer what ever punishment the Captain and crew think fit.

Rule 5 – Anyone striking another crew member shall receive 30 lashes with the whip.

Rule 6 – Anyone that raises their weapon when not in battle or leaves a lighted candle unguarded shall receive same punishment as in Rule 5.

Rule 7 – Anyone losing a finger or toe in a battle shall be given 400 pieces of eight, and if they lose an arm or a leg, shall have 800 pieces.

Visit Pirates' Bay at Charlotteville where pirates had a thriving encampment.

Pirates in the Caribbean
Image is Everything

The British West Indies had become a dumping ground for thousands of so-called malefactors and petty criminals; those politically sentenced or those found guilty of vagrancy were banished by the Courts to work out their sentences on Plantations.

Word got around that a good living was to be had by pirating in the Caribbean and more armed brigands joined forces with the existing buccaneers to create havoc upon the high seas.

By the dawning of the 18th Century, the Bahamas had become a new haven for pirating as buccaneers preyed on merchant ships travelling to and from Virginia. In 1717 English pirate captains Thomas Barrow and Ben Horne declared New Providence (Nassau) a Pirate Republic with themselves as Governors and were soon joined by other notorious rogues like Charles Vane, Calico Jack and the infamous Black Beard.

Opportunist entrepreneurs opened bars, gambling houses and brothels to cater for all their needs and the caricature figure of the pirate came into being, as flush with captured loot, they aped the English dandies with their flamboyant dress adorning themselves with plumed hats, silver buckled shoes, long hooped earrings, massive rings and heavy gold chains encrusted with rubies and emeralds taken from Spanish galleons.

The image of knives clenched between teeth and pistols cocked, arose from the French buccaneers preferred method of boarding ships as they favoured the use of small arms while swinging on ropes over the sides.

In the words of that most lawless Captain, Black Beard the Pirate – *"What ever hand Fate may have dealt us, one thing you must remember......we will not be forgotten".*

Pirates in the Caribbean

THIEF FROM THIEF.....

Some of the best known names in early British Caribbean history includes two knights of that era, Sir John Hawkins and Sir Henry Morgan. They were privateers, i.e. licensed pirates paid by the English Navy from the proceeds of captured ships. Other nations competing in the plunder and pillage business used similar ploys, so these shores were literally awash with mercenaries, rogues & common scallywags including Anne Bonney a female pirate, Black Bart, Calico Jack and the infamous Black Beard, who commanded his own pirate fleet of ships. It was not uncommon for them to rob even those vessels belonging to their respective countries, who were jostling to secure the region for future trade and territorial ownership.

For many years England, France, Spain, Portugal, Denmark and the Netherlands fought long, hard battles on these turquoise seas.

The French ranchers in Haiti coined the term 'buccaneers' from the word *boucan* – a bar-b-q grill used by the original Arawak inhabitants. They preyed upon their Spanish neighbours in Hispaniola and attacked Spanish ships in particular in acts of revenge.

The pirates in the region were so numerous and well armed that they were able to blockade sea ports and over run towns turning them into their private playgrounds.

Pirates in the Caribbean

Pirates in Petticoats

The earliest recorded account of a female pirate was that of a French beauty, Jeanne Belleville, whose husband Lord Clisson was beheaded in 1303. She swore revenge and accompanied by her two ferocious sons became the scourge of the French coast.

Anne Bonny was born to an Irish lawyer and one of his servant girls. She grew up amongst sailors and married John Bonny, running off to manage a tavern where she met 'Calico Jack' and began a life of piracy.

Anne Bonny sailed with her lover, the flamboyant 'Calico Jack' Rackham. Her pirate companion Mary Read assumed the appearance of a man to enlist on a war ship from which she later deserted, before enrolling on the vessel that was captured by 'Calico Jack' and Anne Bonny.

Anne detected that Mary was a female despite wearing men's clothing and being an adept sword fighter. They became firm friends causing the Captain to become jealous thereby forcing Anne to expose the truth in order to save them both.

Eventually they were all captured and put on trial in Spanish Town, Jamaica. The women pleaded pregnancy but were sentenced to death; Mary Read died in childbirth in prison.

Anne Bonny's father paid bribes for the return of his daughter and she disappeared from public life after leaving a chilling reminder for her former lover 'Calico Jack'.

'If you had chosen to stand and fight like a man, you wouldn't have to be hanged like a dog'.

Pirates in the Caribbean

Blackbeard Loses his Head

At 2 metres, Blackbeard was an intimidating figure. He stuck smoking firesticks into his huge beard, an act designed to strike fear and terror into the hearts of his crews and foes alike.

New Providence, later known as Nassau in the Bahamas, was reportedly the most popular hide-out for pirates of all nationalities. The Caribbean was the new economic growth area as sugar became king.

In the Grenadines in 1717, at the height of his powers controlling 400 men and 4 ships, he captured the Concorde a 20 gun French ship. He renamed her Queen Anne's Revenge and added another 20 guns to her fire-power. He overruns a British ship, sets the crew adrift and refuses to accept the 'pardon or death to all pirates' offered by King George. Instead he sailed to South Carolina where he blockaded the Charleston Harbour. The Governor of Virginia hired Robert Maynard an ex-Royal Navy mercenary to bring an end to his reign of terror promising him part of Blackbeard's treasure and providing him with 2 sloops and well-armed troops.

Blackbeard and his men swarmed over Maynard's vessels only to find that the soldiers were hidden below decks. Maynard shot him point blank and he was struck with a cutlass by a soldier. Maynard cut off his head and took it back to collect his reward. News of his death spread to Nassau where Anne Bonny publicly resolved to take his place as the most ruthless pirate in the Caribbean.

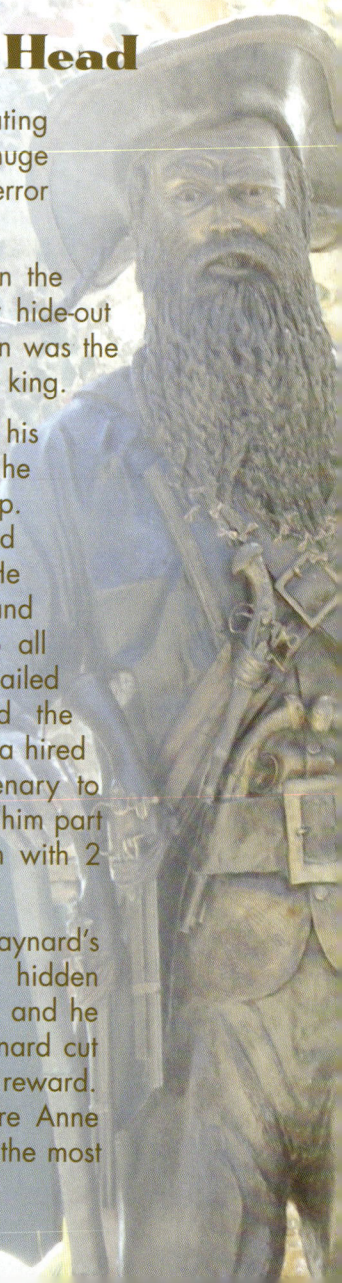

Pirates in the Caribbean

PIRATES IN TOBAGO

Pirates, Buccaneers and Privateers frequented the Islands during the 16th to 18th centuries and thrived due to the lack of law and order.

Privateering was the wide-spread lawful practice of robbing ships and settlements belonging to the enemy. The practice was meant to operate in war time only but continued through peace time. Privateering was utilized by all the nations involved in the bid to break Spain's trade monopoly and in the race to colonise the new world. For example, Spain's laws decreed a five-way-split of any privateers' booty – one for the King, two for the officers and crew, one for the ship's owner and one for the charterer of the expedition. If the booty was captured by the King's ship the last two portions went to the Royal Bankers. Drake, Hawkins, Morgan and Raleigh were all English privateers operating with Royal blessing and investments from within the Royal court. Buccoo Bay, Pirates Bay and Man o' War Bay were old pirate haunts which they used as hideaways and supply depots.

In 1718 Thomas Aristis, one of the last British pirates escaped pursuit by the Royal Navy, eventually landing at Pirates Bay then fleeing into the surrounding jungle. Later, Aristis was murdered in his hammock by one of his crew. The British finally hunted them down and the rest of the pirates were captured and hanged.

For more interesting facts on Tobago see - 'Amazing Tobago Souvenir Map' by Phil Dobson. Available In Gift Shops & Penny Savers Liquor Dept.

Pirates in the Caribbean

Pirates and buccaneers created their own version of modern day Las Vegas in Jamaica's Port Royal, a British array of defensive forts built on a narrow peninsula and the only English stronghold in a huge Spanish zone of occupation in the new world.

Henry Morgan a Welshman, was a paid crew member on the large mercenary force which set off from Bristol in 1654 to harass and rob the Spanish galleons in the Caribbean. They also helped to fortify and built Port Royal, meantime making friends and allies of the real swashbucklers, the mainly French buccaneers who, with other like minded sailors of fortune controlled Tortuga island. Six hundred of them were given residency at the invitation of the Governor as the city grew wealthy, built on stolen bullion when cash-rich pirates spent fortunes in brothels and taverns and traded for supplies.

Henry Morgan mobilised the new pirate residents who formed the main bulk of his force which attacked Spain in Portobello, its stronghold in Panama, carrying off 160 prisoners and 175 mules loaded with loot, which amounted to 10 million pounds sterling at today's value. Port Royal soon turned into the richest and wickedest city in the New World, with over 2,000 brick houses and numerous places of rowdy entertainment and revelry. Its glory days didn't last too long as the English establishments made peace with Spain in 1671, whereupon they both declared war on the pirates in order to make way for their colonial planters to grow sugar cane - the new currency.

The British chose the man with the best credentials in legal piracy and made him the Deputy Governor of Jamaica. When he died, four years before a massive earthquake and fire destroyed this early version of Las Vegas and sunk into the bottom of the sea, Captain Morgan had amassed a fortune of over 100 slaves, vast land holdings and sugar cane plantations.

Pirates in the Caribbean
THE END OF PIRACY

The words 'Buccaneer' and "Filibuster' are exclusive to a specific period in History (17th century) and to the Caribbean. The Buccaneers were French adventurers who hunted wild life-stock and supplied cured and salted meat and skins to smugglers/traders which brought them into conflict with the Spanish authorities who forbade trade with any other nations. They were kicked out of Hispaniola (Dominican Republic) by the Spanish and retaliated by attacking Spanish shipping and Ports whenever possible. They got their name from the method used for smoking meats (boucan), a trick learnt from the original indians. An independant group neither protected nor governed by any Nation, they set up temporary coastal settlements and bartered with passing ships. Their numbers grew considerably and numerous places were made infamous by their association e.g. Port Royal, Panama, Tortola and Tortuga.

Their ranks consisted of motley groups of individuals largely from French, Flemish, Dutch, Irish and British stock but also included castaways, refugees, moroons (escaped African slaves) and Carib Indians drawn together by mutual hatred of the Spanish.

Filibusters, whose name most probably originates from the Dutch 'veijbuiter' (free-booter) meaning free booty, were adventurers commissioned and aided by the other European powers for almost 50 years to prey on Spanish possessions in order to break Spain's monopoly on trade in the Caribbean and the Americas. The lives of these violent and daring men were thrown into confusion and uncertainty when the Nations involved came to trading terms with each other.

England's King issued an amnesty to all pirates who wanted to give up their life of crime - the alternative was death by hanging. They were driven out of the Caribbean by the late 1720's as a result of the eventual supremacy of the combined naval forces sent to hunt them down.

Pirates were rebels and cut-throats - enemies of all mankind. They pursued a life that led to their own destruction but left us a legacy of harrowing and swashbuckling tales.

TOBAGO BRANCH

ANIMAL SHELTER

Tel: 639 - 2567

OUR VISION:

"A stray free country, where animals are treated with love and respect.

OUR MISSION:

To continue our SPOTT (SPAYING PREVENTS OVERPOPULATION IN Trinidad & Tobago)

To implement a spay/neuter programme at temporary clinics where surgeries are carried out by local vets and volunteers vets at a low cost fee.

To get FOREVER homes for our stray dogs and puppies, cats and kittens.

To rescue unwanted animals and attempt to locate owners of lost animals.

To prevent cruelty to animals.

To educate the public on the humane treatment of animals which includes responsible ownership.

Founded in 1968, the Tobago Branch of the TTSPCA is a non-profit organization. Funding comes from donations, legacies and regular fund raising activities. *Donation Boxes* can be found at some stores, hotels and at the airport. Make a donation to our *Acct. #020408593701* Tobago TSPCA at any *REPUBLIC BANK LTD.*

Our Shelter is situated close to the Dwight Yorke Stadium and *visitors are always welcome*.

Clinic hours: Monday - Friday 4pm to 6:30pm and Saturday from 8:30am to 12:30pm

Shelter hours: Monday - Friday 8:30am to 4pm and Saturday from 8:30am to 12:30pm

We depend heavily on the services of *dedicated volunteers* so if you are on the Island and can help we do appreciate your time spent with us, even if its just to walk some dogs.

Membership: We welcome members for the low cost of TT$100

We speak for those who cannot speak for themselves

www.tobagophoto.com

DEC 2009

TRINIDAD & TOBAGO WEST INDIES

What's on...
in TOBAGO®

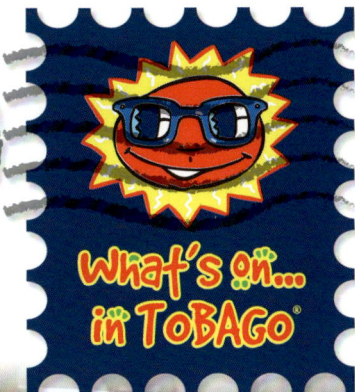

Chapter 10
READERS' PAGES

RECUPERATING IN TOBAGO'S HEALING WATERS

The fairly recent Icelandic volcanic ash episode prompted the recall of the time, some years ago, when a British Caledonian flight didn't arrive in Tobago to take us holiday makers back home as scheduled and we had to be accommodated for the night, courtesy of the Airline.

The anouncement resulted in the passengers going into little anxious huddles. We need not have worried as the Airline's ground Representative had the situation 'well sussed' and within a short time we were taken to the spanking, brand new Coco Reef Resort, whereupon the passengers' collective demeanour changed completely as the prospect of an extra all-inclusive night in swanky surroundings became a reality.

I'd had a hip replacement about 6 weeks prior and while prepared to follow the Doctor's advice regarding air travel, I got around the Airline's Rules on the outbound journey by displaying only one walking stick upon check-in, although I really needed two. I had arranged by phone with our host for a couple of stout walking sticks to be cut and ready for me as well as a driver to ferry us to Mt. Irvine's Public Beach Facility every day. I was hoping that the healing properties of the sea water would help me to make a speedy recovery. The affected leg was so stiff that it dragged badly when walking and it was sheer magic when a Life Guard produced a boogie board in order to help me to exercise the offending limb.

However, after 2 weeks of this wonderful therapy - only possible by using my wife as support when hobbling into the sea, I was disappointed in not being able to bend the leg in a walking motion as I sat in the Airport waiting to board the delayed plan.

She-who-must-be-obeyed, had the good sense the previous night, to have taken the necessaries from our suitcases before checking them in so we were able to have a late lie-in in our enormous bed(room), enjoy a sizeable breakfast and take a final swim in the Resort's blue, seafront waters before being taken back to the Airport for our flight.

AND HERE'S THE MIRACLE OF IT...It was during that final swim, while dangling the stiff leg behind me, as I held on to my wife and kicked with the other, that I suddenly felt the bad leg move and bend and for the first time I was able to simulate a walking motion, albeit hesitantly. It wasn't without a few 'Hallelujahs' that I got on the return flight and ordered a large Brandy to celebrate my good fortune!

One year later, having been offered early retirement because of my hip replacement, we returned to live in Tobago where each year we give birth to the What's on...in Tobago magazine..... another little miracle in itself!!

Starring in the above drama...

* Neil Wilson - the efficient cool-as-a-cucumber Airline Rep. Later to become Tobago's Tourism boss who went on to transform the Island's fledgling tourism industry.

* Michael Baker - the entertainer - who was our host and accommodation provider and his neighbour, our driver. We couldn't have asked for more or better family orientated services.

* Mr. Rawlins - the thoughtful Life Guard who provided the boogie board and monitored my progress. He was the long-serving Life Guard for whom I now make a point of stopping to give a lift when ever I see him on the road.

Don't you just love stories with happy endings? I do...

MY EXCITING FIRST VISIT TO TOBAGO

by Harry Eddington, Norfolk, England

I first came to this 'jewel' island in 1999 for a two-week holiday visiting my daughter and son-in-law who live there.

Having lived in South Africa and Saudi Arabia way back in 1942, it took a time to get used to the heat and humidity once more.

The bird life is so outstanding and colourful; tiny iridescent finches just two inches long, chattering parrots of vivid hues and humming birds all colours of the spectrum to mention a few. There are brilliant green lizards of various sizes and huge Iguanas, as well as geckos scuttling into cracks and crevices and occasionally taking up residence in your home; an absolute haven for many varieties of wild life.

The shallow bays and wonderful silver sands were beyond belief and the views from the hills above Scarborough at the Fort were breathtaking with cannons of yesteryear positioned around the bay and ammunition blocks fashioned out of rectangles of coral - just amazing. Canoe Bay amongst others was a pleasant place to spend time exploring the coasts of this exciting island.

As a last thought, I would like to say that although the tourist trade creates a good amount of employment, perhaps the cocoa, coconut and citrus groves could be revived as these crops grow well on the island and would create a living for more young people.

Please God, let the island remain as I saw it, unspoilt and as nature designed this treasure.

'SHAKIN' MY THANG' IN TOBAGO

By Maxine - Bridgend, South Wales.

In 2007 I visited Tobago to spend 3 months with my relatives at the Hummingbird Hotel in Crown Point.

I attended Carnival J'ouvert, where I mastered the art of the slow and fast wine (nothing to do with the drink). I also went to the pan competitions, which is something that has to be seen live. I also went to a concert called 'Gal Farm' where I saw Machel Montano the Soca King, and other live performances.

I got the chance to see a leatherback turtle laying her eggs on the beach, which is a once in a lifetime experience. Every morning I woke up to the male and female Ant shrike, the tamest of Tobago's birds. On a boat trip I saw dolphins, a turtle and a sail fish, then on to No Man's Land where I had a beach BBQ and on to the Nylon Pool.

Easter weekend was Sunday School where I danced to the pan band and drank lots of Rum Punch. I tried the local fish - yellow fin tuna, red snapper, dolphin (mahi-mahi), flying fish and shark and bake; my uncle taught me to cook lobster. My favourite local foods are Doubles and Roti and I have become accustomed to exotic foods from being here.

Finally, I went to Parlatuvier, Castara and Englishman's Bay. A most memorable experience was meeting the Prince of my homeland Prince Charles and his wife Camilla at Pigeon Point.

READERS' PAGE

We Fell in Love With Tobago

By Egbert & Rose Schiele

After a lifetime of working in Germany, we holidayed in Barbados our favourite destination, as well as taking two Caribbean cruises around 16 islands. On our way home we met Gillian, a Trinidadian stewardess who sent us photos and info. on Tobago which resulted in our first visit in 1993.

We did not regret it; we fell in love with Tobago! At first we discovered Robinson Crusoe's Cave, then Pigeon Point and all the dreamlike beaches of the West Coast; also unforgettable days in the wonderful rain forest and on Little Tobago. In Arnos Vale and Copra House we admired the paradise of nature with such beautiful birds and at Buccoo Bay we saw innumerable fishes. Last but not least, we love the contact with the very friendly Tobagonians who now belong to our circle of real friends and with whom we exchange letters and calls, which are always a great pleasure!

This year we had our seventh visit to Tobago and we noticed a change, unfortunately not to the better. Some people call it progress, but is that a good friend for the future? We saw much more traffic, heard more loud noise everywhere even at midnight and found problems with plastic and other rubbish. For the first time we had a hard disappointment when people showed us that money is much more important than friendship and integrity. Is the greed for money a progress? Of course, money belongs to the daily life of the modern world, but the greatest good is where you live – your paradise Tobago!

Protect it from all bad influences – do it for you and your children!

COMING HOME!
by Maureen Heron

My first impression on arriving in Tobago in 1999 was how much it reminded of Jamaica as a child. People took the time to say good morning or good night (at first I thought it was very strange being greeted with 'good night' at 6 in the evening), and the thought of flagging down a complete stranger's car, getting in and paying him $2-$3 was unheard of. Suffice to say I was completely smitten.

Since coming to Tobago, I have rekindled friendships with people I have known in the UK and made so many new friends, each time I visit I feel like I am coming home. I have also fallen victim to the Tobogonian male charm and I am happy to say survived; ladies beware, the Tobogonian man's chat up lines are like nothing you have heard before!

Despite the number of times I have been to Tobago, I never tire of going to places like Sunday School to people-watch, and of course my favourite, a trek in the rainforest.

Today the 'tourism baby' is growing rapidly and many flights from Europe and America are vying for places on the landing strip. New villas, apartments, and even a huge Shopping Mall are going up fast. You can get all your favourites you thought you had left at home in the Supermarkets.

They had their first Jazz Festival in 2005 and I hear it will be an annual event.

In 1999 I felt as if I had stumbled on a little piece of Paradise that not many people know about - today it's a different story. I think they call it progress.

THE VIEW OF A LONG-TIME VISITOR TO TOBAGO

By Klaus-P Coeppicus

Tobago is one of the last jewels in the World – an Island with beautiful rain forests and surrounded by fish-rich seawaters. It's always been lovely and lovable and is still so today. But there are signs that this idyllic place is becoming more and more endangered. I believe that the environmental mistakes in Europe, Asia and elsewhere need not be repeated here.

The biggest problem I see is the increase in the amount of garbage and how to discard it!

More and more durable plastic (bags, cups, containers) are available to the public every day – **these never rot! This is a time bomb** and work on intelligent solutions to this problem should be a priority i.e. recycling & incineration for example.

Other waste includes various batteries which poison the environment and which should have a central collection place. The beaches become spoilt through lack of bins in which the public can place the ever-present Styrofoam cups and food containers that people inevitably bring to the beach but don't take back home with them. The ocean does the rest! The people need to be conscious of what they have and what they rely on if they want to preserve this treasure for themselves and their children's future.
I have been coming to Tobago since 1992 having travelled widely to India, U.S.A., Europe etc. and found that Tobago is the place I like the most – it's still hard to beat!!

I would like to see Tobago become an example to the World. All those with responsibility for the Island should really do more. Regrets are no help if it's left too late!!

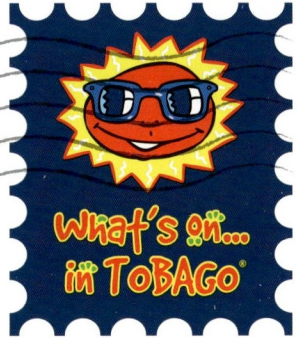

DEC 2009
TRINIDAD & TOBAGO WEST INDIES

What's on... in TOBAGO

Tobago is the only place I have found where I can totally switch off when I'm on holiday. A 'mouse' means only a small furry creature and a 'Blackberry' is a fruit that grows on a bush! After a day getting over the arrival procedures, I can slip into the gentle pace of life in Tobago; as gentle as the waves that just manage to turn over at Pigeon Point beach. If you want things done in a hurry dear visitor, you have come to the wrong place. For me, the greatest charm of Tobago is the slow relaxing pace; and what can you take away with you? Here is a tip — load a picture of Pigeon Point jetty as your screen saver, it will help to keep you cool and relaxed until your next visit!

Steve Rafferty
Norwich, U.K.

Take Tobago home with you®

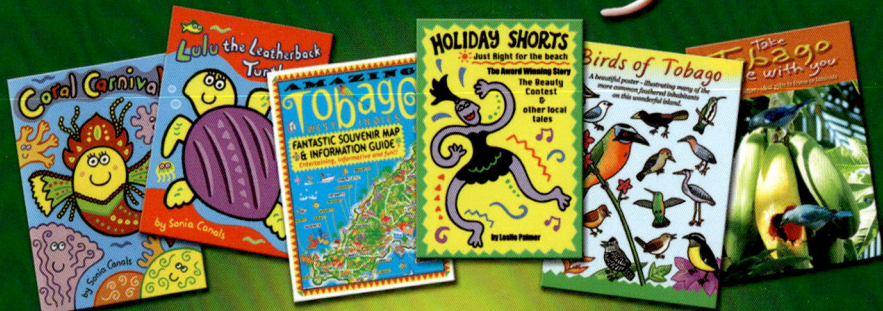

CORAL CARNIVAL - A beautifully executed children's book by Sonia Canals based on the underwater wonderland of Buccoo Reef.

LULU THE LEATHERBACK TURTLE - Sonia Canals' informative illustrations relate the life-cycle of this endangered species in an educational way.

FUN MAP - A unique detailed poster-size Souvenir Map - An ideal gift to frame and hang at home.

HOLIDAY SHORTS - Some powerful short stories in readable dialect - Just right for the beach!

BIRDS OF TOBAGO - A delightful poster by Sonia Canals illustrating many of the wonderful birds of Tobago.

BLUE-GREY TANAGER (BLUE JEAN) - A terrifc action-photo poster of the Blue-Grey Tanager, known locally as the 'Blue Jean', which is a common, medium-sized South American songbird usually found in pairs, feeding mainly on fruits and thriving around human habitation here in Tobago.

Available at all Gift shops island-wide and PennySavers Liquor Department

Published by © London Carnival Lovers
Email - palmertobago@hotmail.com
www.whatsonintobago.com
Editor/Writer - Les Palmer
Designer - Carlene Weekes-Harrylal
                Guess Who Concepts Limited
Production - Rita Palmer

London Carnival Lovers
PUBLISHING